P9-EDD-891

MARITA

This Large Print Book carries the
Seal of Approval of N.A.V.H.

MARITA

THE SPY WHO LOVED CASTRO

MARITA LORENZ

THORNDIKE PRESS
A part of Gale, a Cengage Company

Farmington Hills, Mich • San Francisco • New York • Waterville, Maine
Meriden, Conn • Mason, Ohio • Chicago

Copyright © 2017 by Marita Lorenz.
Thorndike Press, a part of Gale, a Cengage Company.

ALL RIGHTS RESERVED
Thorndike Press® Large Print Biographies and memories.
The text of this Large Print edition is unabridged.
Other aspects of the book may vary from the original edition.
Set in 16 pt. Plantin.

**LIBRARY OF CONGRESS CIP DATA ON FILE.
CATALOGUING IN PUBLICATION FOR THIS BOOK
IS AVAILABLE FROM THE LIBRARY OF CONGRESS**

ISBN-13: 978-1-4328-4444-8 (hardcover)
ISBN-10: 1-4328-4444-X (hardcover)

Published in 2017 by arrangement with Pegasus Books LLC

Printed in Mexico
1 2 3 4 5 6 7 21 20 19 18 17

CONTENTS

FROM THE OFFICIAL STORY
TO THE TRUTH

'Unreliable witness': that was the phrase a member of the Special Committee in the Lower House of the United States Congress who was investigating the assassination of John F. Kennedy used to discredit me when I gave testimony in 1978 under the protection of an order for immunity from prosecution.

I was a witness to events, and more. I was close to the people and places that marked a turning point in political life in the second half of the twentieth century. Wartime Berlin; concentration camp, persecution and pain; Cuba and the revolution; Fidel, the love of my life. As far as the issue of reliability is concerned, that begs the same question of the very authority that trained me to rob and kill, to lie and act above the law . . . I leave it to the reader to decide who is the more trustworthy. I know the truth because I was there. Everything I saw and lived through sticks in my memory and I cannot erase it.

My name is Ilona Marita Lorenz. I was born in Germany in 1939, a few days before Hitler invaded Poland. During the war, I was moved from the hospital at Drangstedt to Bergen-Belsen concentration camp. I survived. Shortly after the liberation, at the age of seven, I was raped by an American sergeant.

In 1959, when I was nineteen years old, I met Fidel Castro. I became his lover and found myself pregnant. In Cuba, I was drugged and forced to undergo what they told me was an abortion but two decades later Fidel introduced me to Andrés, the son they tore from my body on the operating table. Can you imagine what that means to a mother who left the island with an empty belly?

I was pressured by the CIA and the FBI to become involved in Operation 40, a government plot which brought together personnel linked to federal agencies, Cuban exiles, soldiers of fortune and the Mafia to try, in vain, to overthrow Castro. They sent me to Havana with two pills to assassinate him. It wasn't that I failed, like hundreds of others who would later try: it is simply that I was incapable of carrying it out. I don't regret it; on the contrary, it is the thing I am most proud of in my life.

Soon after, in Miami, I fell in love with Marcos Pérez Jiménez, the Venezuelan dictator, and I had a daughter, Monica — Moniquita. When I was deported and our lawyer embezzled the funds Marcos had provided for us, I tried to follow him but I ended up abandoned for months with my baby in the Venezuelan jungle with a tribe of Yanomami Indians.

In November 1963, I drove from Miami to Dallas in convoy. One of my travelling companions was Frank Sturgis (aka Frank Fiorini), who was arrested some years later during the Watergate scandal, a CIA agent, various Cuban exiles, and a man I knew from training sessions for Operation 40 in the Everglades. We called him Ozzie, but he was better known to the world as Lee Harvey Oswald, accused of assassinating John Fitzgerald Kennedy and himself later assassinated by Jack Ruby, who I also had met in the motel where we stayed in Dallas.

I was a party girl with close ties to the New York Mafia, among whom I had several lovers, and there was also someone significant in the police force. I married and had a son, Mark, known as Beegie, with a man who spied on diplomats from the Soviet bloc for the FBI, a mission I took on. Prior to the testimony before Congress, when Sturgis spoke publicly about my role to the press, my world began to fall apart.

I have been a woman in a man's world. I have lied to protect myself and my children and I have told the truth when it suited me. Now I want to leave things clear, perhaps make a certain person who works in the shadows for the US government realise that it isn't worth letting other people make your decisions for you.

I have lived for the last few years on benefits, without a pension, in a ground-floor apartment in Queens with my dog Bufty, a cat, a tortoise and a enormous goldfish that every now and then launches itself in a suicide mission against the glass of the fish tank.

I have never considered taking my own life, although at times I have wanted to die. But dying is easy; the challenge is to live. Sometimes I regret the time lost on missions that had nothing to do with me and faith placed in the wrong men. But I'm proud of having survived war, sexual assault, several attempts to kill me, harassment by the government and a plethora of robberies, misfortunes and betrayals —

including by those of my own blood.

Mine is a story of light and shadow. Some people might think it incredible, but truth can be stranger that fiction. My story is built from memories and documentation, which sometimes portray the seamier side of the official story, one that is not always itself credible.

CHAPTER 1
DON'T SPEAK, DON'T THINK, DON'T BREATHE

I was always destined to be alone. I don't know why.

I should have come into the world with my twin sister, who was to be called Ilona, but when my mother arrived at St Joseph hospital in the German city of Bremen she was attacked by a German shepherd belongings to an SS official who abused her for continuing to see a Jewish gynaecologist until she was full term. My unborn sister died during that attack but I survived and, although I was to be named Marita, they wanted to honour their dead baby and called me Ilona Marita Lorenz instead.

It was 18 August 1939 and only a matter of days before Germany would begin the invasion of Poland and light the match that started the Second World War. They practically threw mama out of hospital to make room for the anticipated wounded and she couldn't count on the help of my father who, at that point, wasn't in Germany anyway: he was at sea, as he was before and after and practically all his life.

Mama was born Alice June Lofland, and she was a woman whose life, even to this day, is shrouded in mystery, with secrets that can never be revealed. She was a true artist of interpretation who I doubt anybody ever truly got to know. She had two birth certificates. According to one of them, she was born on 15 October 1902; the other had the same birth date but gave the year as 1905. Obviously one of the documents is false but neither I nor my family have ever been able to find out which. When I asked my mother where she was born, she always gave me the same answer, the words of a woman who was always extremely cautious: 'It's not important, it's not important.'

The only thing we know for certain is that my mother grew up in the United States, in Wilmington, Delaware. Her family were farmers but she always felt different, even when she was just a child, and when she reached adolescence her parents sent her to New York to a private school in Park Avenue — 'one of the best', as they said. She learned to dance and went into show business, acting in Broadway plays under the stage name of June Paget. Perhaps that was when she began to discover her skill, her talent, becoming a part of a world of masks and personalities that she would never want to or could ever imagine giving up later.

In this period of her life she had a number of affairs that didn't work out, although correspondence and papers that we came across in the family through the years suggest it would perhaps be more appropriate to think of them as romances. One of the men who we know fell hopelessly in love with that beautiful and determined blue-eyed blonde was William Pyle Philips, a noted financier. Alice wanted to have children and this man was not only quite old but was also her cousin so in my mother's opinion this romance had no chance of succeeding. She also wanted to live an independent life and to work in the movies, but, although Philips begged her not to leave him, even offering to organise it so that she could act in her own movie and to open a cinema just for her, it made no difference. Mama spoke fluent French and decided to go to Paris where they were making talkies. She was eighteen or nineteen years old and I think that, apart from advancing her professional career, she wanted to escape the men who pursued her; and there were more than a few because mama inspired genuine passion.

Unsure whether she was running away or searching for something, she left New York on the *Bremen,* a passenger ship belonging to the Norddeutscher Lloyd shipping company based in northern Germany. During the voyage she met the second in command, Heinrich Lorenz, the man who would later become my *papa.* I never called him Papá, Father or Daddy: to me, he was always *papa.* He was a strong man with dark hair and eyes, possibly of Italian descent, and men and women alike were crazy about him.

Papa was born on 8 April 1898 in Bad Münster am Stein-Ebernburg, a spa town in a part of southern Germany famous for its springs. He came from a family of landowners but, just like mama, he found his true passion far away in a world of horizons and rolling waves. For him, the future did not lie in managing the family estate or vineyards. The sea was his life, his dream, a place of freedom and it became his passion. He was already at sea by the age of twelve. When he left the Gymnasium, he signed up on various merchant ships and in 1918 enlisted in the German navy. At the end of the First World War, and after spending a couple of years on a schooner bound for South America, he started working for

16

Norddeutscher Lloyd.

Mama worked in Paris during the 1920s as an actress on some of the first 'talking' films that were produced, still using her stage name of 'June Paget'. After a lengthy courtship my parents were married on 31 August 1932 in the port city of Bremerhaven, Germany, where papa had a house.

Alice hated living in a fishing port so she convinced *papa* to move to Bremen, about sixty kilometres to the south, where she lived comfortably during the early years of their marriage. My father's job paid well enough for her to be able to afford furs and diamonds and they lived in a lovely house with French windows whose glass always sparkled; there were two upper floors, a ground floor, a garage and a garden with a birch tree. Morning coffee, breakfast, lunch and dinner were always served in the dining room, 'never in the kitchen like servants', mama would say, and porcelain cups and silver cutlery were always used. There was a flower arrangement or fruit on the table and hot plates on a serving trolley. After every meal, the table was covered with a lace table cloth.

Mama had domestic help but sometimes she got down on her hands and knees to clean the floor to contribute something to the daily chores so that everything was always perfect.

Alice spoke with pride about the origins of her family on the Isle of Wight; she had explored her mother's side back to the tenth century and the Osborne family. It showed an aristocratic lineage with 'no working class or merchants' featuring in the family tree and everyone was 'cultured, educated and intellectual'. She didn't speak perfect German, but educated herself by reading classic German literature and philosophers like Arthur Schopenhauer and Immanuel Kant, and also studied piano, continuing her general education as a self-taught person.

Papa, who over the years had developed very good relationships through his work, occasionally brought home some of the important figures of the time. On such occasion the street outside would be filled with black convertibles and he wore his dress uniform, medals and sword. However, *papa* spent very little time at home. He was almost always travelling and every time he came back from the sea there was a new child to get to know. In her first pregnancy, mama was expecting triplets but on 17 May 1934 she gave birth prematurely to two girls, neither of whom survived, and a son. He was the first-born and *papa* wanted to name him Fritz in honour of his brother. But during her crossing in 1932, mama had met one of the sons of Kaiser Wilhelm on the *Bremen* who asked her to pay homage to a brother who had died. She acknowledged his request and my eldest brother was therefore baptised Joachim, although I have always called him Joe or JoJo.

After JoJo, on 11 August 1935 Philip — Kiki — arrived in the family and he was the one child in particular who developed a passion for music and the arts that mama made such an effort to instil in all of us. In the choice of name for his second offspring *papa* didn't have much of a say either because when mama left Philip, the cousin who had been so besotted with her, the only thing that she left behind apart from a broken heart was the promise that if she ever had children she would baptise one of them in his honour.

On 9 October 1936 my only sister was born; I have always had the most complicated of sibling relationships with her. *Papa* wanted her to be called Elsa but mama decided on Valerie. For her last child, mama was also left to her own devices in choosing a name and ignored the name my father wanted for me — Anna.

A Family of Spies?

While Europe and the rest of the world stared into the abyss, my parents began to move in a perplexing universe which I never understood. I never knew for certain what political beliefs my parents held. As the years have passed I have only discovered a few details, behind which lies a tangled web of espionage and dirty tricks; seeing how my life panned out, this must have been in my DNA.

In 1938, for example, *papa* and the captain of another German ship were detained as 'material witnesses' in a plot investigated by the FBI, a 'spy hunt' that the *New York Times* described in its day as one of the largest seen in the United States since the First World War. Established in 1935, the network infiltrated German secret service agents as crew on German ships so that they could get to the United States. Once they had settled they helped American soldiers, who had started to collaborate with Germany, to pass information and steal secrets from the army and the navy. The hairdresser on the *Europa,* Johanna Hofmann, was arrested in February when *papa* commanded the ship and was, according to the investigators, the key person in the network, the link for Americans recruited by Germany, and who

20

weren't known to each other, to pass on information.

Papa and the captain of the other ship were detained on 3 June and it made the front page of the *New York Times*. But the next day, according to the same newspaper, they set sail for Germany without any problems. On their departure they were seen smiling and waving goodbye to Leon Torrou, an FBI special agent, and Lester Dunigan, assistant to the Director of Public Prosecutions. Although I have no way of proving it with absolute certainty, I would say that that was when my father started to collaborate with the US government, when he began his counter-espionage activities. If nothing else he was at least an informant and there is documentation that suggests this was the case.

War broke out on 1 September 1939, when I was only two weeks old. At the start of the conflict, *papa* was a crewman aboard warships and other vessels that navigated round Greenland and visited meteorological stations. In 1941 he was recalled to take command of the *Bremen,* a ship that would become famous as one of those intended to be used in Operation Seelöewe [Sea Lion], Hitler's planned invasion of England. The idea was to camouflage the ship and hide in it the cannon and tanks they would instigate the attack but the operation was never carried out. *Papa* received an urgent call on 16 March informing him that the *Bremen* had been involved in a fire at Bremerhaven. The official version was that a disgruntled fifteen-year-old cabin boy, who had a grievance against the owners, had started the fire. He was sentenced to death and executed. Yet it was rumoured that the British secret service managed to infiltrate the German navy and blew it up, frustrating the Führer's plans, so he had personally ordered the boy's execution in an attempt to save face.

Mama was arrested shortly after the explosion on the *Bremen,* the first of several occasions when she ended up in the hands of the Gestapo. They interrogated her under suspicion of having collaborated with the British secret services in planning the attack, but they had to release her because they couldn't prove anything. In spite of investigating her family background to see if she had any Jewish blood, the Gestapo instead discovered her lineage and even congratulated *papa* for having married someone of noble birth; but they didn't stop watching her. That should also have put him under suspicion. At least that is what *papa* feared.

My brother Joe remembers an occasion when my parents had an intense conversation at home with an admiral who wanted them to join the growing opposition to the Nazi regime led by disaffected military officers. *Papa* had declined: the risks involved in such an operation to someone married to an American would be too great. Years later, on seeing a photograph, Joe identified the naval officer as Admiral Wilhelm Canaris, chief of the Abwehr, the German military intelligence service, who was accused of co-operating with the Allies, convicted of high treason and executed in 1945 at Flossenbürg concentration camp.

Although they didn't join Canaris's network, there are indications that mama and *papa* did carry out counter-espionage activities. On 1 May 1940, for example, they were both at a party in Guatemala organised by the German Embassy, which was based in Tegucigalpa in Honduras; they weren't present, like the other guests, to take part in a celebration but were on a secret mission: to spy on Nazis for the Americans.

Mama felt the pressure of always living under suspicion and tried to escape from Germany but she felt anchored in Hitler's

Europe; although she wanted to escape, she couldn't because her priority was always to protect us — my two brothers, my sister and me. She tried to take all four of us to the United States and wrote to the Swiss consulate with that objective in mind. However, when the Swiss got in touch with their American counterparts they replied that she could return but we children couldn't because we were German. She refused to abandon us and her attempt to take us out of Germany was also the cause of a new arrest and further interrogation, the accusation this time that she had communicated with the Swiss consulate to pass information to Washington.

Chanel No. 5; The Smell of Phosphorus

Although I was very young then, I have some indelible memories that are still with me today, flashes of places, episodes and sensations that frightened me or made me feel emotional. This keeps alive my personal history and the dear people who are no longer here or are far away, in some cases physically, in others emotionally, which is worse. One of the most enduring memories I have of my mother is the scent of Chanel No. 5 and of her making a fire to keep us warm and melting snow so that we had water. I recall every corner of the basement of the house where we hid during bombing raids and, above all, the smell of phosphorus. Mama made my brothers and my sister sleep fully dressed on their beds in a large room in the upper part of the house so they were ready to come running down to the basement as soon as the sirens sounded. When the bombs began to fall, we could see the flashes through the black curtains that covered the small window. We spent interminable hours in that reinforced basement which was next to a room that led out to the garden just below our balcony.

Joe had a British army helmet, one of the steel ones that mama and *papa* must have found somewhere. For Philip they had made a different helmet, a saucepan lined with socks so that it wouldn't be too uncomfortable. Mama also made me a doll out of socks that I hugged the entire time I was down in the basement and she sang to me to keep me calm. The place smelled intensely of bananas that hung under the stairs; someone must have given them to my father as a gift, taken from ships coming from Latin American that the Germans had intercepted. Sometimes all we had to eat, as my sister Valerie remembers with disgust,

25

were rotten vegetables and a little rancid butter.

In those moments of terror the basement was much more than a refuge to us. You had to keep absolutely quiet, not a whisper, and that's when I came up with a mantra that I still repeat to myself in times of danger: 'Don't speak, don't think, don't breathe'.

Survival depended on more than avoiding bombs falling from the sky. There was also danger in the streets, in the shadows of the German soldiers we heard passing above us, the steel of their boots ringing with every step they took, for me always a threatening sound. It was imperative that we maintained absolute silence so that they didn't hear us. Less of a concern was that they would hear our screams or our frightened crying, more that they might find our shortwave radio which mama had hidden behind a false wall so that she could listen to the BBC at nine o'clock in the evening and find out how the war was really going. To have such a radio at that time was considered high treason and in fact mama was accused of that one day when Joe turned the radio on to listen to some music. This attracted the attention of one of the passing German soldiers and he came into our house. Fortunately, it occurred to mama to explain who *papa* was and she argued that he needed the radio to know the conditions at sea and the weather forecast before he sailed. She must have been convincing because this time they didn't arrest her. Nor did they confiscate the radio.

Mama was unquestionably a brave and determined woman, the dominant influence in a family that knew how to stay together. When he got one of his rare shore leave permits, *papa* would come home for three or four days and then return to sea, leaving everything in Alice's hands, from paying the rent to making sure we had something to eat. She was the one who saved the house when, in 1941, a fire after a bombing run almost destroyed it. She was also the one who helped the French and British during the war, although that led to her being arrested, interrogated and abused on more that one occasion.

My brother Joe remembers how on his fifth birthday he went to his first violin lesson and walked by an area near the house were the Nazis kept French prisoners who collected our rubbish. When he returned and told mama, she said that next time he should stand in front of them and say: 'Je suis Américain. Vive la liberté.' Mama started leaving food and other things they asked for at the door of the house. They asked for all sorts of things, from cameras to radios, and couldn't always get everything they needed.

She was without a shadow of a doubt a strong woman, a real fighter, committed body and soul to a battle in which the only successful option was survival, whatever the cost. One day, for instance, during the bombing, a Pole who was very drunk came into our house. In his inebriated state he must have thought that mama, with no man around to protect her, was vulnerable, an easy victim, and he tried to rape her. He threw himself on her and started to assault her but after a struggle mama managed to push him off her. She gained some time and was quick to take advantage of the obvious state of her attacker by tempting him with something else to drink. The man, who had obviously had quite a lot to drink already, accepted, not realising that the bottle she gave him was filled with a floor cleaner. He died in our basement. Alice grabbed him by the feet, dragged him up the ramp to the garage and deposited him near the house in a bomb crater which was filled with snow. Years later, when we talked about that terrifying incident, the only thing she said to me about what happened was:

'He deserved it.'

During the war she had to make some of the most difficult decisions a mother can make on her own. In 1944, at a time when the Russians were advancing on the city, German officials came to the house to demand that Joe be sent to a school in Meissen. With so many soldiers dying in the conflict, Hitler knew that the future of Germany depended on its youth and he needed to educate them and give them discipline. There was no option but to send her son away for the sake of the future because failure to do so would leave her without a ration book; this, as they make clear with threats, would mean that she wouldn't be able to feed her three other children. With no alternative or way out, and with no right of appeal for twenty-four hours, Alice had to let her eldest son go and to this day he remembers vividly her taking him to the train.

Like the consummate actress that she was, mama packed Joe off, telling him that he was going on an exciting journey, one on which he would make new friends, and she promised him that his life was going to be much better. She constructed an elaborate story of a happy world and told my brother all this without allowing her smile to slip for

29

a second, peppering the conversation with phrases full of excitement and delight, telling him all the time how much she would like to go with him because he was going to have such a good time. Her only task was to try make JoJo feel comfortable although he must have been terrified at the thought that he might never see his mother ever again.

After that, mama sent Philip to live with a piano teacher who hid and left Valerie with the Tantzens, our neighbours. The father of the family was a dentist to the SS and also a portrait photographer who had filled the shop windows of Bremen with images of mama and her four children, symbols of the ideal German family.

After this enforced separation in order to survive, she and I were the only two left. Sometimes we had to leave the house and, as I was still very small and couldn't run as quickly as mama, I remember her pushing me into a trench and throwing herself on top of me to protect me. That trench was the very same one that would later be occupied by British soldiers who stopped to brew tea in a lull in the fighting and Scottish soldiers who sometimes played their bagpipes. It was incredible to listen to such sounds between bombing raids and they left me confused, unable to tell which world I was in.

There was also a bunker close by in which to shelter when the Allies were bombing but going there wasn't a good experience. Our German neighbours didn't want mama. They didn't like her and they made it clear on many occasions. I have always believed that they were envious of her beauty, but she was a foreigner and therefore the enemy, in practical terms. She didn't have a Nazi flag to hang out on 20 April, Hitler's birthday, and once they denounced her to the Gestapo for that.

On many occasions the Germans revealed that they knew about everything she did during those years of struggle, barbarism and resistance; a story of small, individual deeds that, thanks to memories and letters of gratitude that arrived after the end of the war, we can keep alive. On one occasion, for example, she saved a pilot who had been shot down. Finding him amid the rubble, she took him home with her, hid him in our basement and then lent him one of *papa*'s uniforms so that he could escape. She also doused incendiary bombs, secretly fed the prisoners in the neighbouring forced labour camp and let a few people listen to the radio so that, as a result, they could organise the resistance better.

German Children Don't Cry

During the war, mama was arrested on several occasions, aside from when she was denounced by neighbours or when German soldiers found out about her collaboration. By good luck, they never knew about her most serious acts of betrayal, only the minor ones, and although she wasn't exempt from mistreatment and torture, she was eventually freed because she was the wife of a German citizen.

However, when I was five years old they arrested her again and on this occasion, tragically for me, things were different. I was left on my own and I became very ill with typhoid fever so they took me to Drangstedt, near Bremerhaven, to facilities under the control of the SS which served as a children's hospital. That was my first incarceration and it was the most painful one. I have never in my life suffered such heartache as I felt there.

In Drangstedt there was a group of large buildings and huts situated in the middle of a dense pine wood surrounded by wire fences, with a swimming pool which had a large swastika on the bottom. It was a cold, dark spot and you could hear the sound of dogs barking constantly, and gunshots. Although there was a kind of communal dormitory where boys and girls slept, children like me from mixed marriages between Germans and foreign nationals, I was left on my own in room 29. My bed had bars and there were also bars on the windows. I was my own worst enemy because I was so confused and felt so homesick that I couldn't stop crying, and every time I cried the nurses hit me and shouted,

'German children don't cry!'

They gave me terrible injections with a huge needle; there was forced feeding; castor oil and beatings . . . However, worst of all were the ice baths. They put me in a bath full of icy water and put my hands under the tap, letting it run and run, and I thought I was going to die because after a while I couldn't feel my body, or anything in fact. Even today, the memory of those baths gives me nightmares.

The life of tears, homesickness, heartache and suffering became routine for me until on day they took us all away from that place. They put me with the other children into the back of a lorry and I only remember that I had a scratchy grey blanket, although it wasn't enough to protect me from the cold so we all huddled together to try to keep warm.

Hell On Earth

I was so ill I don't know exactly what happened but they moved me to Bergen-Belsen concentration camp. Everything there smelled, everyone looked dead, nobody smiled, nobody spoke and the only thing I could do was cry. Cry, although doing so didn't relive the fear, the anxiety and the discomfort. Cry until there were no tears left to cry, until our bodies surrendered to the injustice we were suffering.

In the large hut that I was in, the same one, I later discovered, in which Anne Frank died, there were children from the very young to adolescents and we were all very cold, so, as in the lorry that had transported us there, all we could do was to huddle together. Some of us were already half-dead. We chewed black bread and sometimes there was soup made from beans and some other vegetable and it was a lucky day when it was your turn to get a potato. That was all we had.

I didn't know it at the time but my mother was in another part of the same camp. It was always very difficult for her to talk about her experiences during the war, although in her writings which I have seen over the years and in conversations with her I discovered that Josef Kramer, the camp commandant who would later be known as the Beast of Belsen and who had also been at Auschwitz, had refined a system of psychological torture while he dished out physical abuse, above all to a woman who he constantly called 'an American pig'.

'The nurses were particularly pleased when they abused and mistreated me,' mama recalled in her writings and memories that I kept together with her poems and other written accounts. 'One of them, Sister Elfrieda, hated all Americans and me in particular [. . .]. At four o'clock every morning, she pulled the sheet off me and emptied a bucket of cold water over my feverish body. Then, lifting me up by the hair, she slapped my face and pinched my breasts until I fainted in her arms.'

Joe found mama close to death in the camp. He had returned home from the school in Meissen by himself. He had witnessed the bombing of Dresden on 14 February 1945, a moment of war that, with his prodigious memory, my brother remembers as 'the most extraordinary sight, the twilight of the gods: one hundred and eighty degrees of burning sky, sudden blasts hurling bodies up several kilometres into the sky, the air sucked from an earth where people died engulfed by the infernal temperature . . .'. After that, JoJo thought his return would be a celebration for the whole family that he hadn't seen for months. As each day passed he was less able to contain his happiness as he recognised familiar places: first the Schwachhausen area, then our street in which he had played all his life, and finally the building at number 31, our house, with its birch tree, the garden with a swing and a small sand-pit. Joe pictured mama running out to meet him, followed by Philip, Valerie and me . . . He took a deep breath on the porch in front of the main door, from where he could see a Mexican blanket hanging on the wall, and pressed the bell. There was no response. He waited and pressed it again. Still silence. He must have rung the bell ten times or more until, with a sense of horror, he realised there was no one there. While he thought about what to do, Mrs Tantzen came out of the house to the left and called to him enthusiastically, 'JoJo!'. At first she didn't answer when he asked about where we were. Joe stayed the night with the neighbours who had been looking after Valerie; he insisted on asking of mama's whereabouts at breakfast and they told him that she had been interned in Bergen-Belsen. My brother was only ten years old but, as he said, by that age 'I had already learned to take control of things and, instead of crying, I knew what I had to do'.

The next day, with fourteen marks in his pocket, he caught the train and forty-five minutes later he arrived in a wooded area where he thought he could see some tracks which he started to follow, thinking they would lead to the concentration camp. He saw two German women in black working clothes emerging from a different path which didn't lead to the main entrance and so he asked them if he could get into the camp unseen on the track that he was following.

'No, you can't,' they confirmed.

'I have to. My mother is here,' he replied.

The expressions on their faces changed. One of them stroked his head and said 'poor boy'. The other answered:

'Is your mother a Jew?'

When Joe said that she wasn't, that Alice was American, one of the women turned to the other and said:

'That's a little better.'

They told him that they worked in the camp but used the short cut to save themselves a two-kilometre walk. They told him where to find a stretch of fence that he could lift up to slip through, where there was a piece of wood to cross a large pond and where the dispensary was located. They thought his mother might be there. They also gave him two instructions:

'For God's sake don't tell anyone how you got in and for goodness' sake don't look to the left when you get there.'

Joe set off but found himself unable to ignore the second instruction and glanced to the left. What he saw, and he can still remember it clearly to this day, was 'a strange mountain, like a hill about three metres high'. He quickly realised that it wasn't a mound of earth but something more sinister — massive towers of skeletons, arms, legs and skulls all piled up . . .

He walked on and when he reached the three steps that led up to the entrance of the dispensary, a nurse asked him who he was and what he was doing there. He replied that he was looking for his mother, Alice June Lorenz, an American citizen.

'The American,' the woman said and took him to his mother, passing rooms full of people lying on the floor.

Alice was lying on a kind of rickety old bed; her head had been shaved and she was almost unconscious. Joe leaned over her fragile body and when she realised he was by her side she opened her eyes and managed to say:

'JoJo, you're here — where have you come from?'

He told her how he had got back from Meissen and asked her why her head had been shaved.

'One of the men here has got it in for me, but don't worry, it will grow back.'

My brother then asked about Philip, Valerie and me . . . Mama simply replied:

'I hope we'll all see each other soon.'

The nurse urged my brother to leave because mama was very weak but, above all, because the woman must have had a heart after all and knew that it was dangerous for this child to be there. Nobody entered the camp and stayed there willingly. That danger presented itself in the shape of a uniformed colonel in high leather boots and a white overcoat who, as the nurse had warned, started to ask questions about who this boy was and what he was doing there. Turning directly to Joe, he questioned him about our parents, if he was a member of the Nazi Youth and other details about his life. Even at the age of ten my brother knew how to give the right answers, telling him things like how *papa* had broken the British blockade three times to reach Greenland.

But if anything saved Joe it was his quick wit in answering the officer when he asked him about what he had seen in the camp that had made an impression on him. When the nurse heard the question, she began to cry and my brother knew that if he mentioned the mountain of corpses he would never get out of there so it occurred to him to say that he had seen blood in a pond. The official then told him about a violent dog to explain away the presence of the blood. He believed, or acted as if he believed, my brother's innocence and let him go, signing a pass so that the guards on the gate would allow him to leave.

Three or four days later Joe received a call from the camp doctor telling him to come and collect mama. Her condition had deteriorated to the point where they thought she was dead and they had moved her from the hut to deposit her with the other bodies. But while she was there someone noticed that she was still alive. Mama told Joe that she had had an out of body experience where she saw herself walking towards the light. Although she tried, she couldn't go because she knew that she had to come back and look after her four children. With that

40

strong determination to survive, and for reasons that we haven't been able to explain completely, the people in charge at Bergen-Belsen let her go. Joe went to the concentration camp with Mr Tantzen, the photographer and dentist to the SS who, throughout the war, had hidden his car in our garage. They collected mama and that part of the nightmare came to an end.

Little by little, back at our house in Bremen and under Joe's care, mama recovered. One day, Major Davis, a coloured US military officer, showed up at the house. News of the help mama had given to the Allies during the war must have reached him because he knew who she was and where she lived. He had come looking for her to ask her if she would become his personal assistant in Bremerhaven. After the Allied victory, when they divided Germany into different zones, the British retained control of the North Sea but left the city of Bremerhaven as a port enclave for the Americans and Davis needed someone he could trust who spoke both English and German. Mama was delighted to accept but refused to leave Bremen until they found me. Finally, with the help of the military, she did.

They found me in the spring after the

Germans left a camp consumed by death and disease and the British liberated it on 15 April 1945. When they entered, I was hiding under a rickety old wooden bed, the place where I usually secreted myself for fear of being beaten, but my feet were sticking out and an ambulance driver saw them and pulled me out. When he got me out, I fell to my knees; I was full of worms and covered in lice and bruises and I weighed twenty kilos so I couldn't stand up by myself. I was almost dead. Almost. I was one of two hundred surviving children.

After rescuing me, they took me to an old SS hospital in the country where, as in the swimming pool at Drangstedt, you could still see a large tiled swastika on the main lobby floor. I was looked after and they gave me the clothes belonging to a girl who had died so that my mother would see me looking half-decent when she came to get me.

The End of One Nightmare and the Beginning of Another

She didn't take long to do so. Mama arrived at the hospital with Major Davis. Sitting next to each other on the back seat of the jeep he was driving, we went home and at last we were all together again; Mama, Joe, Kiki, Valerie and me. Soon after, we moved to Bremerhaven.

Only *papa* was absent. A prisoner of war in the United Kingdom during the conflict, he had been released and returned to Germany but the Americans wouldn't let him live with us in the house they had given mama. I imagine they had doubts about someone who had been an officer in the German navy, although there were also indications that he had helped people who were being persecuted; that, at least, was a possibility because when his ship had been torpedoed in 1943 by the British and they were processing the survivors to place them in prison camps, including a family with children, he convinced them that someone in the German navy was helping people escape from Germany. Even though it would almost certainly have been *papa* who saved those people, they didn't let him live in the house we had moved to although sometimes he came to see us on the sly. Valerie remembers one of the days she saw him there.

'*Papa!*' she shouted.

'Shhh,' he replied. 'No one can know that I'm here.'

Although I didn't have a happy childhood, such moments after the family was reunited left me with happy memories. I was so small and so traumatised that I didn't even recognise my brothers and my sister. Joe and Kiki looked after me, protected me and tried to give me the childhood that had been stolen from me up to then: they took me ice-skating, they taught me to ride a bike and they played with me. The situation was very different with my sister Valerie, who I'd been separated from for much of my early childhood, even though I tried as hard as I could to be a sister to her. She insists to this day that our relationship was a normal one but I believe that, to her, it was as if I appeared out of thin air. Valerie was small and neat, and then I turned up, wounded, different and scruffy. She never let me play with her or her friends and, even though I hate to say it, she behaved like a rat.

In spite of my brothers' efforts, I felt so isolated. I didn't know how to play or smile and I started mixing with a group of street children. Obviously, we hadn't got over the war; we were still survivors of a sort, or at least I couldn't get everything that had happened to me out of my mind: the bombings, the terror, Drangstedt, Bergen-Belsen . . . With my friends I spent my time committing little acts of violence and we stole food, sweets and cigarettes from American trucks which we could sell, pawn or swap. My brothers had started to go to the American Dependent School. I had made it clear that I would be the black sheep of the family. My mother tried to instil in me the American way of life and I . . . well, I just wanted to be a little girl.

One day, I was invited to play at the house of another girl who lived in the same street as us, Oldenburger Strasse. Patty Coyne was the four-year-old daughter of John J. Coyne, a sergeant from the United States. Mama dressed me with a white ribbon in my hair, a pink dress and some smart shoes instead of the boots I always liked to wear. And off I went. It was 26 December 1945, the day after Christmas.

The sergeant took us to the basement to play hide and seek and switched off the light and Patty and I hid. He found me first and then his daughter. He turned out the light again and we played another game in which he acted as if he was a big wolf howling in the darkness. I was hiding but he found me and grabbed me. Patty was still hiding. The sergeant told me to lie down on the carpet and when I refused he pushed me till I fell on my back. Then he threw himself on me. He weighed a lot and hurt me. I tried to get up but he was so heavy that it was impossible and he forcibly held me down. I tried in vain to get him off me, to push him away, but he lifted my dress and put his hand on my body. I pulled his hair and hit him in the face, I cried and shouted at him to stop and to let me get up but he covered my mouth with his hand. Then he tried to put one of his fingers inside my body. All the time he was rubbing himself hard between my legs and then he rubbed even harder for a long time in the place that I peed from. I cried and shouted and he covered my mouth with his hand again and squeezed my neck with the other. All the time he was howling and shouting as if he was a furious beast to frighten me, moving himself back and forth, hurting me.

I was terrified, helpless, and I think that I may even have fainted. I felt an unbearable pain and I crawled up the stairs. I was bleeding and I realised I had sticky fluid between my legs. I don't know how I found the way to the back door but I left and crawled home.

An employee who worked for mama saw me and she was surprised at how dirty I was and commented to one of the other housemaids that she couldn't believe how a girl would have stained her clothes and pants like that simply while playing. Mama also saw my pants with the bloodstains on the bathroom floor but she thought I had just cut my legs.

Five days later, on 31 December, I finally told mama what had happened. To her horror, Valerie, who was then ten years old, told her that Sergeant Coyne had tried to attack her the day before at a Christmas party for children. On one of the games, he had also succeeded in throwing her back on the carpet but she had managed to bite his finger and kick him in the shins, which helped her get free. She went up to the living room where Mrs Coyne was with two women and a soldier, picked up a chocolate that they had given her and her hat and coat and went home. Mama had given her such a telling off for coming home in such a filthy state but she was too frightened to tell her why.

On 31 December, when mama finally realised what had happened, she immediately took me to a clinic for a vaginal examination. Dr McGregor told me that I had a perforated hymen and several lesions but as he didn't have the necessary equipment to determine if I had been raped, he suggested we go to the emergency hospital for more thorough tests. That experience, four days later, was horrible, nothing but doctors and pain. The doctors spoke in English and Ger-

man and my mother was absolutely hysterical when they confirmed it was rape. She
threatened to kill the sergeant, and cried
and screamed, although it was clear who
the perpetrator was, 'Who could have done
something like this?'

I know she wasn't trying to hurt me —
she was desperately upset — but she
shouted at me as well, asking me why I
hadn't been able to get away. I wanted to
tell her that I couldn't. He was too big . . .
And I was a seven and a half year-old-girl.

They sent me away to an island, Norder-
ney, in the North Sea, to recover, where I
had to spend two or three quiet days with a
nurse. When I returned home, I told my
mother that the woman had touched me
inappropriately. Perhaps mama thought that
it was just my vivid, traumatised imagination; perhaps she didn't want to embark on
another battle against yet another enemy
when we still had to fight a battle against
Coyne in a military court. She let the nurse
go in any case.

I would see the man who raped me once
more during the judicial process. I was
frightened to death and couldn't bear to
look at his face, so I started to shout when I
saw him. My mind was functioning as what
it was, the mind of a child, and I was

frightened, thinking that he would be released or that he was going to jump over the table and grab me again and I just wanted them to tie him up. The sergeant pleaded guilty. He was convicted and sent back to the United States to a prison in the north of New York state. However, the court learned that not only had he robbed me of my innocence and tried to attack Valerie, but he had also raped two other young girls who lived nearby.

It was without doubt a horrible experience but I don't believe it marked my life apart from giving me a few nightmares. My brothers say that in those days I went from a happy and mischievous child without a care in the world to being sad and introverted, a change that can be seen in photographs that Kiki took during that period. After that, I didn't talk for almost a year, I didn't trust people in uniform, I had lost my innocence and gained a fear, a dread of complete darkness. I didn't smile, I didn't play with other girls, I didn't trust anyone and I didn't have any confidence. I just wanted to curl up into a ball.

After the concentration camp and the rape, I couldn't see the point of going to school either. I felt incapable of sitting at a desk, taking orders from people who spoke in English and who I could barely understand. I didn't want to be there, I didn't understand the two worlds they made me live in, being both German and American, without really knowing in my youth and confusion which one I belonged to. It was just like in the war; when we were at home with mama we were American and externally we conformed to what we were supposed to be — German. Everything confused me and I only had my own set of rules. Before long I was expelled from school.

Sailing with *Papa*

I didn't care if I went to class or not. The truth is that I wanted to go to sea with *papa,* to be with him. I was as restless as the wind and wanted to be a sailor and not be tied to any one place. He had opened my imagination, telling me stories of distant places, beautiful islands where oranges grew on the trees, places where there was peace and beauty. His stories made me think that not all the world was as cold and hostile as I had experienced and suffered up till then. He filled my head with dreams and I dreamed.

The first ship I sailed on was the *Wangerooge.* My father was the captain. I loved every millimetre of that boat, I adored its sounds and the sounds of the sea, the smell of petrol and the water, the turbulent winters and the storms. More than anything, I loved being near *papa,* a man who was sweet, soft and wonderful with me and who represented the protection I wanted after everything that had happened. It might sound like an exaggeration to say that, for me, he was a god, but that was the kind of child I was. On board he let me do what I wanted and I was happy to be just another member of the crew, peeling potatoes, eating with the sailors . . . That, for me, was my favourite school, one where I understood the discipline and one I didn't mind being in, a classroom on the waves and beneath an open sky with the best teacher. It was a floating school in which I learned about the winds, the currents and fish. And also about life because *papa* taught me that when you have the tiller in your hand, the boat is yours; you set the course, you face the elements and you sail towards the destination that you have set; no one steers but you.

I learned the lesson, although perhaps not how he would have wanted. When *papa* couldn't let me on to his ship for some reason, I sneaked on board as a stowaway; once I felt enough time had passed on the voyage and we were far enough away from the coast, I came out of my hiding place, frozen, shivering, hungry and prepared for the surprise and the initial ruckus but also knowing that I was ready to sail and conscious that the captain wouldn't turn round to take me back to port.

Nigger Lover

During those years I was in the custody of mama as she and *papa* had divorced in 1946 by mutual consent. Although their marriage wasn't perfect, the legal separation took place essentially to make sure that they would let mama take her children to the United States. However, I have to admit that in the first years of the war, when *papa* came home during his brief shore leaves, he would sometimes go out with a couple of German women. He didn't do it to have extra-marital flings but because he found more understanding or empathy with them, given the situation in the country, than he did from his own wife. Years later, my parents would marry again but in 1946 their divorce was essential for legal reasons. Finally, in 1950, my mother was given permission to take us out of Germany.

We travelled on the *Henry Gibbons,* a ship that transported military personnel from

Bremerhaven to the United States. We arrived in New York at Brooklyn Pier on 1 May 1950. Mama thought that someone from her family would give her some help on our arrival but no one did. As with so many other things in her life, she was forced to rely on herself.

To begin with, for example, we were taken in by an uncle of hers who lived in Peter Cooper Village, a housing complex built to the east of Manhattan which was part of post-war urban planning to provide homes for war veterans. You could feel that our presence there was inconvenient and, from that point on, it was clear that her relatives were going to help her as little as possible. Then we went to Bradenton, near Sarasota in Florida, to Aunt Lucy's, a cousin of mama's married to a major in the army who worked at the Pentagon. That was when I began to hate Florida, a state which has played a prominent part in my life and I would return there continually over the next few decades.

My brothers went to high school and mama enrolled me in elementary school. But it didn't suit me; I felt very lonely, I had no friends, I spoke with a German accent, the other children hated me and I hated them; in my eyes they were uncouth and provincial. The only things I liked in Florida were the watermelons. The only thing I did was cry all day, saying that I wanted to go back to Germany and be with *papa*. The dreamer and sailor he had raised reappeared constantly and joined forces with my rebellious spirit. At that time, when I was just a teenager, I tried to escape and even planned to steal a ship that was carrying water, bread, mangoes and oranges.

I was a wild child and I must have been a nightmare for my mother who finally sent me to New York when *papa,* who was then in command of another ship, the *Gripsholm,* came to the United States. I travelled from Florida by myself and I waited for Captain Lorenz on Pier 97 used by Norddeutscher Lloyd. I was happy when I saw *papa* and he was happy when he saw me. I think he felt lonely as well.

In 1951, mama was transferred from Florida to Washington, DC, to work for the United States Army Criminal Investigation Command, the CID, so they sent us to the capital. After going to a couple of houses on Monroe Street, we ended up at number 1418, not far from the area dotted with embassies and diplomatic legations that was known as Embassy Row, where I rode my Schwinn bicycle or played on the roller skates that mama had bought for me.

I was a young girl with long plaits when I went to the Bancroft Elementary School where I got As, particularly in History, and where I felt that I knew more than the other children, perhaps because of all the things that I had experienced. Then it was time to go to intermediate school where I witnessed and personally lived through one of the darkest chapters in the history of the United States: the outbreak of racial tension that accompanied the increasingly unstoppable fight for civil rights which demonstrated the bitter racism of a society where many still refused to recognise equality and end centuries of oppression.

I got on very well with black children and I didn't understand the hatred towards them. The ones who seemed horrible to me were the white people. One day I went to school and there were crowds which I walked through while the white people yelled at me 'nigger lover, nigger lover'. Only that day, Angela, the daughter of an Indian diplomat, and I had gone into the classroom where our teacher, Marie Irving, who was black, was by herself. Some teenagers appeared in the classroom and started overturning desks, attacking the three of us repeatedly. One of my teeth was broken in the attack and the only thing I could find to use in self-defence was the flagstaff bearing the Stars and Stripes; I started waving it around and I hit boys who were attacking us; thanks to this, they were forced to leave the classroom, although not without first verbally abusing us.

Mama was always very loving towards me, very understanding, sweet; she hugged me endlessly, sat me in her lap and called me 'my little survivor' and repeatedly told me 'I always said I wouldn't leave you'. But that day she was furious. She insisted that I stop fighting with everyone and told me that I wouldn't go back to the school. So I never went to high school, although later, as my sister Valerie remembers, I made a fake certificate using hers and by rubbing out her name and putting in my own I 'graduated'.

Mama decided to take me to work with her in a navy building on 14th Street where I spent several months delivering letters, taking messages and eating with her. It was a routine that I liked and it also gave me the opportunity to get to know a lot of military personnel and their way of thinking.

I was a happy teenager. But then they sent mama to Addis Ababa in Ethiopia, one of

56

many trips, jobs and missions she undertook for the Pentagon about which she would say nothing at all; not then, not ever. With her departure, my life became one of constant activity again. My brother Joe went to college and I should have gone to live with him but I wrote to *papa* to see if he would let me go to Germany and he agreed. When he arrived in New York on the *Lichtenstein,* I travelled there and embarked with him, setting course for Bremerhaven.

Return to Germany, Return to the Sea

In Germany I spent time at *papa*'s house on Leher Tor Street in Bremerhaven carrying out domestic duties and I enrolled at the Berlitz School to learn some Spanish. But I really wanted to go to sea with him, so I went back to the bad old ways and I sneaked on board at the start of one of the *Lichtenstein*'s crossings. When we returned to port, he sent me to live with Uncle Fritz, but I was really unhappy and *papa* had a change of heart and agreed to take me with him on his voyages. So began the sea adventures on the *Gripsholm* and then on the *Berlin,* the first of the passenger ships to sail on the regular route between Europe and the United States after the war and which also sailed on cruises to the Caribbean and

West Indies in the winter.

When *papa* became captain of the *Berlin,* sailing with him became a religion, and not just for me. Many of his friends and acquaintances joined him on these cruises, shopkeepers on New York's Upper East Side and German émigrés who had moved to the East Coast of the United States. As captain, *papa* had become a talismanic figure and the sailors held a superstition that when he wasn't present something would happen, a myth that grew when, for instance, three members of the crew were caught by a wave when he was on shore leave. Not only was he considered a good chief by the personnel on board but he was also loved by the passengers. Among those loyal to Captain Lorenz were some very distinguished people, among them Louis Ferdinand, Prince of Prussia, Willy Brandt, later Chancellor of Germany and winner of the Nobel Peace Prize, Theodor Heuss, the first post-war president of the Federal Republic of Germany, who also taught me how to play chess, and members of the Leitz family, founders of the Leica camera company and who saved thousands of Jews during the war.

On those crossings we went to the San Blas archipelago in Panama, the Dominican Republic, Haiti, Colombia and Santo

Tomás. Cuba, situated more to the north, was to be the last stop on the return journey to New York and sugar was loaded on board there which was then exported to Germany. After various trips, Havana had become my favourite destination; the music was marvellous, the people were agreeable and attractive and the rice with beans was delicious. I loved the mamey fruit, iced coconut and the Tropicana Club. *Papa* certainly never let me go out alone.

On the ship I always got up very early to the smell of fresh bread rolls that were baked each day. Like me, there were other people who had grown up on *papa*'s ships, such as two teenage boys born in Bremerhaven who were chosen for their good looks to open the lift doors on the *Berlin*. They once sneaked a tiger cub on to the ship to the fury of the crew and the passengers. They were called Siegfried & Roy and years later they became famous in Las Vegas with their magic show and entertainment with big cats.

I always looked forward to the next island we would call at. I read everything I could about each place, so as to get to know its history. *Papa* also taught me things about the places, explaining the peculiarities that made each island different.

'The only thing they have in common is revolutions,' he would say to me. 'Presidents don't last long in this part of the world. It is the usual way of life: kill each other and take control of the country.'

CHAPTER 2
FIDEL'S LITTLE GERMAN GIRL

At the beginning of 1959 a revolution that *papa* had told me about, and which the world had been waiting for, finally broke out. Five and a half years after the failed attack on the Moncada Barracks on 26 July 1953, and after imprisonment, exile and regrouping in Mexico, his return to Cuba in 1956 on the *Granma* planning the resistance and then the battle from the Sierra Maestra, the revolution led by Fidel Castro triumphed. He was the new champion in the fight for Cuban independence and he took over from the national hero at the time, José Martí.

Fulgencio Batista, the dictator who had ruled Cuba between 1933 and 1944, returned to power on 10 March 1952 following a *coup d'état* after exile in Florida and installed a regime of tyranny, arrest, torture and murder. He made a desperate escape in the early morning of 1 January 1959 after ensuring he took the lion's share of a fortune amassed during his years in power and estimated at between $300 and $400 million.

The United States had held colonial and imperial aspirations for Cuba since the beginning of the nineteenth century and had been fully involved in the transformation of the island until, in 1898, it split from Spain in a conflict which Washington described as a 'splendid little war'. Now, that great power could do nothing either to stop the triumph of the revolution or the law graduate who immediately became an icon, an emblem and an example for all the other revolutions against dictatorships, social injustice and poverty that were sweeping through Latin America. However, at the end of 1958 the director of the CIA, Allen Dulles, informed President Dwight Eisenhower that Castro's victory might 'not be in the interests of the United States and American industries and businesses' that had transformed Cuba into a kind of plantation. The world was warming to this 'extraordinary' young man, as the *New York Times* called him. The newspaper, like so many others, confessed that it was impressed with a victory which had succeeded 'against the odds', thanks to a 'courageous, tenacious and intelligent' fight. The United States government could not be the only one to stand back. By 7 January, a day before Castro made his triumphant entrance into Havana, Washington had recognised the new government of Cuba and had appointed an ambassador. However, the pace of diplomacy and politics didn't put an end to the nervousness within the Eisenhower government, nor among American industrialists or within the Mafia, which was watching its empire in the Caribbean collapse.

That small island, situated barely 145 kilometres off the coast of Florida and on which the eyes of the world were focused, was to be the last stop on the *Berlin*'s cruise through the West Indies, having set sail from the United States on 14 February. We docked in the port of Havana late in the evening of Friday 27 February. There was excitement among the passengers but they showed no nervousness at all and the ship's programme went ahead as normal, a tour starting from the port to get to know the nightlife in Havana — which had gained some notoriety as the wildest in the entire western hemisphere — music in the Alligator Bar on the *Berlin* and morning mass on the 28th at eight in the morning.

On that Saturday, those passengers who

wanted to were able to take an excursion to explore Havana, the jewel of the Caribbean and a tropical paradise of which American tourists dreamed. As usual, some stayed on board with the crew who had to prepare for the return journey north which we would be embarking on that night.

At one point during that day we saw a pair of launches approaching the *Berlin* full of men armed with rifles. It was a sight that frightened some of the passengers and their voices betrayed their fear that we would be boarded. *Papa* was sleeping and I decided that I should take command. I went to a lower deck to be closer to the water and the gangway to speak to the occupants of the launches. When they arrived alongside our ship I saw that there were a lot of them, bearded and armed, dressed in military uniform. However, my attention was caught by one of them in particular, the tallest. He was very close and I liked what I saw a great deal. His face fascinated me.

I waved and asked:

'What do you want?'

The tall man answered.

'I want to board the ship, take a look around.'

I spoke a little Spanish and he a little

English but at that particular moment we communicated mostly in sign language.

I am Cuba

He was the first up the gangway and I saw that he had a cigar in his hand and more in the top pocket of his shirt. I really wanted to see his eyes. I will never forget the first time I beheld that penetrating stare, that beautiful face, that wicked and seductive smile, and I can say that I started to flirt with him right then. I was nineteen years old. I found out later that he was thirty-two.

He introduced himself in English.

'I am Dr Castro, Fidel. I am Cuba. I have come to visit your large ship.'

'Welcome. You are in Germany,' I replied, trying to convert the ship into a neutral territory that wouldn't spark mistrust.

'These are Cuban waters. Cuba is mine,' he replied.

The passengers were obviously worried and frightened by the weapons that the *barbudos* [bearded soldiers] carried so I decided to try to get them to put them down in order to allay the passengers' fears.

'Lay down your weapons, you don't need them here,' I said to him.

There was no need to discuss it further and Castro lined up all his men on the deck

and they left their rifles on the floor, lean-
ing against a wall, an image that was im-
mortalised in a photograph on board, the
first in a series that would create a record of
the hours that followed. Although the *barbudos* had put down their weapons, Fidel
still carried a pistol and I insisted that he
leave that behind as well. He refused, simply
saying 'don't worry'. Then he asked about
the captain and, with a fearlessness that
surprises me even today, I replied:

'He's sleeping. I'm the captain now'

I offered to show him around the ship and
we went towards the lift which was full of
people. Once inside, Fidel touched my hand
and an electric charge ran through me. He
looked at me and asked me my name.

'Ilona Marita Lorenz,' I said, suddenly shy.

'Marita Alemanita [little German girl],' he
replied. It was the first of many times that
he would lovingly call me by that name,
'Alemanita'. He squeezed my hand then
quickly let it go before anyone could see.

It was clear to me from our first meeting
that he exercised a great charm over people,
over everyone. I was no exception and I
decided not to let go of him or be separated
from him. We walked very close to each
other and I wanted to show him the heart
of the ship, the boiler room where the

engineers were bewildered when they saw me with this group of Cubans in military uniform. Warming up the engines for the return journey was due to continue for a few hours and as the pistons moved in their rhythmic, mechanical choreography Fidel remarked that they reminded him of mambo dancers. These were some of the few words I could hear because the noise was deafening. But it didn't matter whether he said anything to me or nothing at all. He put his hand on mine again on one of the handrails from where we looked into the boiler room and, for me, that was more magical than any words.

From there I took him to the kitchen and he was very polite to all the chefs dressed in spotless whites. I also showed him the new refrigerators that *papa* was so proud of and which guaranteed that all food cargo from the different stops in the Caribbean arrived in Germany in perfect condition. I showed him the stores and the staircases. Fidel seemed to be genuinely amazed. What was amazing to me was to walk around with him and, wherever he could, he took my hand, which aroused feelings in me that I hadn't felt before and which I liked a lot.

We went through the first level, which was tourist class, and when we arrived in the first-class area I showed him where my cabin was. Then he said:

'I want to see it.'

I opened the door and, at that moment, he took me by the arm and pushed me inside. Without any ceremony, he embraced me and kissed me. There had been only one other occasion when someone had tried to kiss me. There was a boy who *papa* wanted me to marry, the son of one of the families that owned IG Farben, the chemicals conglomerate that supplied the Nazis with the pesticide Zyklon B that was used in the gas chambers to wipe out millions of people. When I was with that boy in Bremerhaven, whose name I can't even remember, and he tried to kiss me, I didn't like it and I didn't let him continue so Fidel's kiss was my first proper one.

I was in a state of shock and also very happy and that kiss was the prelude to my first sexual experience. We didn't make love in the cabin but we explored every inch of each other's bodies — I felt his body and he discovered mine. I was worried that news of the arrival of Fidel and his *barbudos* on board had already spread through the ship and I didn't want anyone to start asking questions, so after a further passionate embrace I insisted that we had to move on.

When we managed to unravel our bodies from each other, we left my cabin. My hair was a complete mess and all my lipstick had worn off. I know that the *barbudos* knew exactly what was going on but they didn't say a word. Fidel and I didn't say anything either. There was no need to. What happened between us was something I was never going to forget. I don't think he would forget it either.

We went to the Alligator Bar where the passengers danced and enjoyed the music every evening. While he drank a Becks, I found out how much he liked German beer. At that moment my father called me over the loudspeakers and I knew that *papa* had woken up. He never called me Marita, as mama did, but always referred to me as Ilona. Without a doubt it was *papa* who broadcast the message in German.

'Ilona, come to the bridge immediately.'

I knew I couldn't disobey so I headed towards the bridge with Fidel beside me and the *barbudos* following us. As we approached, he said that the bridge was to a captain what the Sierra Maestra had been for him: the Sierra Maestra was the mountain from which he had organised and commanded. We continued walking and talking when suddenly he pushed me between two lifeboats. He pretended he was looking at the view but he embraced me and kissed me again and I felt like I was in heaven once more.

I didn't have much time to think about what this all meant or of the consequences because we were soon on the bridge. *Papa* was already there, surrounded by other members of the crew, in his uniform with the gold rings, looking like a little Napoleon as I introduced 'Dr Fidel Castro Ruz'. They greeted each other with a firm handshake and started to talk. *Papa* spoke fluent Spanish but I couldn't follow all the conversation, although I understood enough to hear Fidel recount how he had wanted to come and see the enormous ship after spying it from his room at the Havana Hilton, the hotel which housed the revolutionary headquarters after its triumph and which they had renamed the 'Habana Libre'. He joked as well, telling *papa* that he had his own vessel and talked about the *Granma,* the eighteen-metre-long boat designed to carry twelve passengers in which Fidel and eighty-one fellow revolutionaries made history in November 1956 with an agonising and almost unsuccessful crossing from the port of Tuxpan in Mexico to Alegría de Pío. After that, the decimated group of practically unarmed individuals took refuge in the Sierra Maestra and brought about a change and, ultimately, victory after a struggle that would not have been possible without the help of the peasantry.

They were chatting and joking while they were served wine, caviar and champagne. They exchanged reminiscences and spent hours in conversation while I came and went. I know that *papa* was aware that every time I came back in Fidel stared at me, although he didn't say anything at the time. The two of them seemed to get on very well and established a good connection which oozed confidence. Fidel confessed that he wasn't a politician and found the challenges and responsibilities of all the promises he had made overwhelming and that now he had to deliver them. He mentioned the sugar, and that in 1958 Cuba was selling 58 per cent of its sugar production in the US market, which was also the destination for two-thirds of the remaining exports and the source of three-quarters of all Cuban imports. They talked a lot about gambling and the Mafia, whom he wanted to expel from the island, and about tourism and the dangers that he knew he faced. He even asked *papa* if he would stay on the island or return as director of tourism, an offer that the captain politely declined. Then I heard *papa* say:

'Do whatever you want but don't fall out with our brother in the north.'

'Captain, Rockefeller owns three-quarters of the island and that isn't right,' replied Fidel, referring to the famous American family and owners of the United Fruit Company, a company that also owned plantations in Colombia, Costa Rica, Jamaica, Nicaragua, Panama, the Dominican Republic and Guatemala.

Papa reminded him what had happened in Guatemala. After the nationalisation in 1954 by Jacobo Arbenz's government of much of the land owned by the United Fruit Company, and despite the unfounded fears of Washington about Guatemalan links with communism, the CIA helped to organise and carry out a coup which installed a military dictatorship. I heard *papa* saying to Fidel, 'there are ways of doing things and ways of not doing things. You are in a very delicate position. You must be very careful.'

They carried on talking till it was time for dinner and then we went to the first-class restaurant and sat at the captain's table. Lots of tourists came up to us, wanting autographs. Regardless of all the hospitality and the claims on his attention, Fidel still had time to hold my hand the whole time under the table and to look at me and he even politely asked if he could keep me on the island to help him with translation work. *Papa* refused, explaining that I had to go back to school. He and mama were tired of my nomadic life and wanted me to start putting down roots. They had enrolled me in an accountancy college in New York, the Merchant Bankers Secretarial School.

The *Berlin* had to sail that night and my time with Fidel came to an end. I didn't want to leave but it was time to say goodbye. I gave him a match-box from the bar on which I had written the telephone number of the New York apartment where I was going to live with my brother Joe, who was studying at the School of International Relations at the University of Columbia. As soon as he took the box of matches I knew I would see him again. I didn't know when or how, but I was convinced that he wanted to see me again too. We looked at each other and smiled knowingly. I had never felt anything like this before. I had fallen absolutely and hopelessly in love and although it is usual to say you feel butterflies in your stomach when you fall in love, elephants in my stomach would be a better way to describe what I was feeling at that moment.

I went with Fidel on to the deck where they had left their weapons and I confessed to him,

'I'm going to miss beautiful Cuba and I'm going to miss you.'

'I'm going to miss you, but I'll be thinking of you and I'll see you again very soon.'

When he left I approached *papa*.

'I like him,' I said.

'He's very pleasant and very intelligent,' he replied. 'I think he's a good person but he's going to need guidance. He isn't a politician. He's a revolutionary.'

Loving Every Minute with Him

I went to the highest point on the ship where I could see all of Havana. The view was beautiful with its spectacular bay, all the lights of the city twinkling, but I couldn't enjoy it. As the launches receded, growing smaller and smaller, I felt increasingly sad.

That night, we started our return journey and when we arrived in New York *papa* continued on to Germany while I went back to the apartment where I would be alone with Joe as mama was on her way to Heidelberg with the army. It was assumed that I would go to classes at the academy and continue my education but I spent my time reading everything I could find about Fidel, including articles written by Herbert Matthews, a journalist on the *New York Times* who had interviewed him in the Sierra Maestra. My head was still in that cabin or between the lifeboats, with those eyes and that body. With that man.

I soon learned that I wasn't the only one who was enchanted by our meeting. Joe went to a seminar about Latin America at that time which was organised by a professor at Columbia, Frank Tannenbaum. Raúl Roa Kourí was there, the son of Fidel's new Minister for Foreign Affairs, who was about to be named ambassador to the United Nations. Raúl Roa spoke to the students about agrarian reforms that Fidel was about to embark on in Cuba. This led to a discussion on what had happened in Guatamela and at the end of the class, when the ambassador asked to speak with my brother, it wasn't exactly to carry on the conversation about politics but to give him 'a personal message from Fidel'.

'Your sister is always welcome in Cuba as a guest of the state,' he said. 'We will look after her as well as we can.'

Roa wasn't joking and I knew that Castro had fallen in love with me when, just three days after I had returned to New York on the *Berlin,* the telephone rang in my brother's apartment while I was making Jello. When I picked up the receiver I heard the international operator telling me I had a call from Cuba. I dropped the dish and it broke into a thousand pieces. Then I heard Fidel.

'Is that Alemanita?'

'Yes! Yes! Yes!' I replied shouting and quite unable to contain my excitement. 'You called! You didn't forget!'

'I'm a man of my word,' he replied with that voice that made me melt inside.

He asked me if I'd like to go back to Cuba. I was very excited and without a second thought I answered, 'Yes! Yes! Yes!' I couldn't think about anything else other than being with him again.

'I'll send a plane for you tomorrow,' he said.

I was overcome with excitement and immediately started to pack a suitcase and a bag. I knew that I couldn't ask Joe for permission because, if I spoke to him and tried to convince him, he wouldn't let me go to Cuba. So I decided to say nothing and the following day I simply took a drawing pin and pinned it onto Havana on a map of Cuba that was hanging on the wall. I left the house on 4 March 1959 with three Cubans who had come to collect me. There was a captain, whose name I don't remember, Pedro Pérez Fonte and Jesús Yáñez Pelletier, who was known as 'the man who saved Fidel' because in 1953, when he was military supervisor at Boniato prison in Santiago de Cuba, he had reported an attempt to poison the lawyer who was imprisoned after the attack on the Moncada Barracks.

All four of us went to Idlewild, the New York airport that is today called JFK, and we boarded a Cuban Airlines plane which had no other passengers but us and a single air hostess. They gave me a copy of a magazine called *Bohemia,* a coffee and a crème caramel, and so began a trip that would change my life forever.

We landed in Havana where a jeep was awaiting us. When I asked where we were going, they just answered with two words that for Cuba and for me over the next few months meant everything.

'To Castro.'

No one said anything about the route either but I recognised the hotel when we arrived: the Havana Hilton where I had had breakfast a couple of times with *papa* on the cruise stopovers on the island. I never thought that those previous trips would end here and, even less so, with Fidel. I was

77

thrilled that I was going to see him, to be with him, and I wasn't frightened at all. I just had a great sense of anticipation that I tried to control and to behave myself like a proper young lady.

My heart was beating so fast I could have flown. We took the lift to the twenty-fourth floor. We walked down a corridor full of *barbudos* sitting on the floor, wearing the same uniforms they must have worn when they came down from the mountain and which I saw them wearing on the ship with their rifles. Everyone was very cordial and polite to me as we walked past and then we reached room 2408, Fidel's suite, which was connected with others occupied by Ernesto 'Che' Guevara and other people in his main team such as his brother Raúl or Camilo Cienfuegos. Yáñez Pelletier opened the door. We walked in and he said:

'Stay here till Fidel comes. He will be here soon.'

He opened the curtains and the door to the balcony and left me there alone, looking round the room. The first thing I remember is the smell of cigars. I went out on to the balcony and was amazed by the views over the entire port of Havana. The *Berlin* wasn't there this time, an absence which made me feel sad and lonely. I was a little melancholy thinking about *papa* who hadn't the faintest idea that his baby was disobeying him and had set out on another adventure, without him this time.

In any case, I couldn't go back because I had taken a path that I couldn't retrace. All I could do was stay and wait for Fidel so I occupied my time looking round the room. I saw, for example, a bazooka sticking out from under the bed a bit and I tripped over it. There were weapons in the bottom of the wardrobe, uniforms in laundry service plastic bags, a pair of military boots and another pair of formal boots made in England. Looking around, I also saw portrait photographs of Fidel that other people had taken. I saw things that he had brought down from the mountain — letters, boxes and a couple of straw hats, bottles of beer, Romeo y Julieta cigars in their tubes, underwear and boxer shorts. I went into the bathroom to wash and I saw there was aftershave lotion but no razor or razor blades. I smelled the pillow on the bed and noticed that you could still see the imprint of Fidel's body on the mattress. Later, I would find out that he didn't sleep much.

I heard voices then the key turning and there was Fidel.

'Alemanita!' he exclaimed. 'See? We're

together again. I have missed you so much.'

He was strong, 1.91 metres tall and around 100 kilos, he took me in his arms and swung me around. He smelled of Havana cigars. We kissed and sat on the edge of the bed, holding hands.

'I'll stay a few days,' I said.

'Yes, yes,' he replied. He said 'yes, yes' to everything.

He poured some Cuba Libres and signalled to Celia Sánchez, one of his closest aides, to leave us alone, telling her that he didn't want any calls put through or any interruptions of any kind. We were alone and I started to hear the sounds of 'Piano mágico', a new record at the time that became a classic and one of Fidel's favourites. I was a bit frightened but soon started to feel the effects of the rum and I looked at him in amazement. Love was right there, in front of me. I could touch it and feel it and it was just how it had felt the first time in my life a few days earlier on the *Berlin*. I didn't care about who he was to the rest of the world or about politics and I didn't care about ideology or all the other things I had been reading incessantly for the last three days in New York. I only cared about him. My man. Fidel.

We started to explore each other's bodies,

expressing a pure and wonderful love, sweet, nothing crazy, caressing and embracing each other. He was concerned that he was too big for me but I told him not to worry, that everything would be all right. We made love and worshipped each other. He called me 'my love' all the time and I kept saying 'I love it, I love it'. I guess I shouldn't have said it but I did say it and I kept saying it often, giving myself up to passion which, thank God, has no boundaries. In that bed and that room, I discovered that Fidel was a sweet and gentle man, so unlike the frightening image that some Americans had started to give him. He was a complete romantic when he was in a good mood.

After we had sex that first time, we leaned over the balcony together and, as he embraced me, he said,

'Everything you can see is my Cuba. I am Cuba. You are now the First Lady of Cuba.'

At that moment, by his side, I felt like a queen.

In those first few moments together he told me that I would stay there with him and he tried to make me feel at home. He tried to calm the nerves and fears that I began to feel when I thought about my family's inevitable reaction, even though they didn't know that I had gone to Cuba by myself. Fidel calmed me down, saying he would talk to *papa*. They had a very good relationship, even though their meeting had only lasted a few hours. What Fidel didn't explain to me when he went is why he did it and why he left me on my own. It was an abrupt farewell which was only the beginning of a pattern that would become very familiar. At that goodbye, the first of many, he explained that Celia would bring me things to do and I could spend my time organising and sorting mail and he made it clear that he didn't want me to go anywhere on my own because I would find everything I needed in the hotel: a shop, restaurant, laundry service . . . So without more ado, he left and I stayed there, not knowing what to do other than have a shower. I listened to the radio, continued looking round the room and at his records and toys which were made in England.

The following night he came back and I thought that this was how it would be: he would spend his days working, I would spend my days waiting and at night I would have his entire attention. But I was wrong and soon he told me he would only come 'for short periods of time'. Part of the reason he gave for not even spending the whole night with me was that he made the majority of trips to explore the situation on the island at night, so as to be able to move around quickly and avoid the crowds. I realised, however, that he didn't sleep much and also that he came and went as he pleased, a pattern that I soon got used to. In any case, I loved every minute there and I didn't feel lonely. I obeyed him and never complained. In those first few days, I was submissive and patient. I learned to be calm and to wait, always to wait.

Sometimes he spent the whole night with me, but only rarely. It was really difficult because the whole world made demands on him for meetings, conversations, trips, negotiations, discussions . . . I tried to be as understanding as I could, although I confess that sometimes I was annoyed about the excessive demands of the rest of the world. Above all, I didn't like it that he was surrounded by other women because it was obvious that Fidel could have anyone he wanted. He wasn't short of offers. I was frightened of the competition. He made me jealous, talking about other women, although he was only joking.

Being in the Habana Libre started to take its toll on me. Sometimes it was exasperating and I began to show signs that I was fed up with the situation. So Fidel decided to give me carte blanche to go out with Yáñez Pelletier on assignments that his personal bodyguard had to carry out. On such outings I could wear the honorary uniform of the Movimiento 26 de Julio [26th of July Movement] which Fidel had given me so that I didn't look out of place, as I would have done if I had continued to dress like a tourist. It was Yáñez, for example, who took me to the house of an elderly couple named Fernández, who I went back to see several times. They were close friends of Fidel and his English teachers. They left me there for the afternoon and the elderly couple and I talked, had a coffee and sometimes I went out with Mrs Fernández to buy things or I learned to cook with her. On other occasions, Pedro Pérez Fonte, whose wife was pregnant, collected me and we went to Varadero to spend the day on the beach. I spent time with Celia, organising the mail and books or taking telephone calls . . . I wanted to be useful, not to sit around waiting for my lover, and she and I laughed together, particularly when we read the letters from actresses and countless other women who wrote to Fidel declaring their love for him or wanting to meet him. Many of the letters included photographs and I looked at them and I made comments such as 'ugly

American', a display of jealousy that made Celia laugh and which demonstrated my own insecurity which today I have no problem in recognising. I didn't want Fidel to see those messages from so many admirers.

His mail was also full of petitions: hundreds of people who wanted to start businesses, Mafiosi asking favours, many asking him for clemency for someone who had been arrested or to release someone from prison. The volume of correspondence was such that Fidel was overwhelmed and it was impossible to answer all of it so he signed a large 'F' on official white paper and left it to Yánez or Celia to fill in the rest.

In the moments that Fidel and I spent together, as well as making love we also talked about politics. Although I didn't have any particular leanings or any firm ideology, I understood that there was something fundamentally wrong when peasants with hardly anything had to scrape a living next door to houses and mansions with servants. It was a miserable situation that reminded me of my wartime childhood with people melting snow to be able to have water or with just a few rotten root vegetables and a bit of rancid butter to eat. Fidel talked to me about the injustices in the plantations with near naked workers earning a miserable fifty cents a day. He loved to explain his ideas about agrarian reform, the confiscation of land that was poorly or illegally cultivated and a fairer division of property that would not only break the yoke of colonialism but would also help to combat unemployment.

A Golfer Called Dwight Eisenhower

Agrarian reform was precisely the kind of political measure proposed in Cuba that terrified the United States. Because of that fear, as well as Washington's dread of the expansion of communism in Latin America and the growing influence of the Soviet Union in this hemisphere, they planned the first trip that Fidel made to the United States in April 1959 and I accompanied him. It didn't even cross my mind to let him go on his own because I was besotted with him and very jealous. As well as that, the eleven-day journey wasn't only Fidel's first visit to the United States but also my first opportunity to go back and see my family after my hurried departure the previous month. I didn't know if mama would be there because I had been sending her letters to a military PO Box without an address and *papa* was in Germany while they were working on the construction of the new *Bre-*

men, which he was to captain. But at least I could see Joe who, at that moment, was in his own little world surrounded by his diplomatic friends, fighting to carve his place in the world and begin a career in that field.

Fidel arrived in the United States not by way of an official invitation from the government, which he didn't ask for and wasn't given, but at the request of the American Society of Newspaper Editors, although during his stay in the country there was considerable interest from the government. In fact, when he landed in Washington he was received by Christian Herter, a high-ranking official from the State Department who organised a dinner for him the next day. As well as that, he was seen by members of the Foreign Affairs Committee, the Senate and also the House of Representatives. He was to have the opportunity to have a first meeting with the Eisenhower administration although, to his fury, it wasn't the President who received him in Washington but the Vice-President, Richard Nixon. It was arranged that the President would be absent from the capital and, to add insult to injury, he went to play golf in Georgia with some friends. Fidel interpreted that as a flagrant lack of respect and he was furious.

Inspired by the words of wisdom that *papa* imparted on the *Bremen*, I advised him to be patient. I tried to reason with him, to help him and convince him that he shouldn't take it personally but it was useless. He felt poorly treated, useless and misunderstood. Looking in the mirror, he said:

'But I am Fidel. How could they do this to me?'

Because he was so furious he didn't decline the meeting and, accompanied by Yáñez Pelletier, kept the appointment which took place on 19 April in Nixon's office in the Senate. Fidel left there annoyed and offended, remarking that they 'hadn't even offered me a cup of coffee'. He was deeply disappointed by the Vice-President who he didn't like at all either as a person or as a politician. In contrast, initially Nixon didn't have a bad impression of him. In a report which he edited after the meeting, or so it was thought when this document was officially released in 1980, the Vice-President wrote: 'My evaluation of him [Fidel] as a man is quite ambivalent. What we can be certain of is that he has indefinable qualities which make him a leader. Regardless of what we think of him, he is going to be an important factor in the development of

88

Cuba and very possibly in the development of Latin American affairs generally. He seems to be sincere; he is either incredibly naïve about communism or he is under a communist discipline — my guess is the former. However, because he is leader, we have no option but to try to guide him in the right direction.' That analysis didn't make any difference: in spite of such a frustrating meeting for Fidel, his attitude towards the American government changed radically and Nixon didn't hold those relatively friendly sentiments for much longer.

We went from Washington to New Jersey and then to New York where we stayed at the Statler Hilton, today the Pennsylvania Hotel situated next to the railway station in the heart of Manhattan. Just as in the nation's capital, the citizens of the Big Apple threw themselves into the arrival of a man who was unquestionably charismatic. Fidel was often surrounded and cheered on by crowds, although he was also abused by pro-Batista and anti-communist supporters. Some iconic images remain from those days when he never removed his military uniform, such as his visit to Yankee Stadium or the Zoo in the Bronx were they took one of my favourite photographs. In it, he is exchanging an intense stare with an enormous caged tiger, an image that, for me, reflected his whole character and was a perfect metaphor for him, a majestic and fierce animal who understood the tragedy of the loss of liberty and not only the kind which comes from being behind bars.

He also gave press conferences, speeches, talks and interviews, occasions in which he liked to define himself as 'just a lawyer who took up arms to defend the law'. He explained his plans for industrialisation in Cuba. He denied that there were mass executions on the island as the American press had now begun to claim. He played down the delay in holding elections or insisted on distancing himself from communism. 'If there are any communists in my government, they have no influence,' he said one day, stressing that neither he nor his brother were communist, nor was his sister-in-law, Vilma Espín.

On a personal level, for me the trip confirmed absolutely that wherever he went hordes of women surrounded and pursued him, something that drove me mad. He enjoyed making me mad, joking, pointing out how many women he had around him and saying they all wanted him. I had only one response.

'They don't love you as much as I do.'

Fidel left New York on 25 April and travelled to Boston, Montreal and Houston before going to a summit in Argentina. I decided to stay in the United States for a few days and pay a few visits. I knew that Joe wouldn't let me go back to Cuba on my own a second time so I told him that I wanted to go to Florida to see one of the daughters of the Drexler family, friends of *papa*. Although he did so reluctantly, my brother gave me permission but instead of staying in Florida I went back to Havana from there. Obviously, JoJo didn't trust me very much in those days after I had gone the first time in March so he persuaded a friend of his who was going to Mexico to follow me to Cuba. This was El Sayed El-Reedy, a young diplomat who worked at the United Nations for the United Arab Republic [also known as the United Arab States or UAS], the state which was created from the union of Egypt and Syria between 1958 and 1961. When he arrived on the island, he took a room on the same floor, twenty-four, of the Habana Libre where I was staying. When Fidel found out he was there, he went to the room and banged on the door until El-Reedy opened it in his pyjamas. He shook him and asked him what the hell he wanted with 'la Alemanita'. I could hear the commotion from my room and I heard El Sayed shouting:

'I'm a diplomat! You can't do this to me!'

His protests served no purpose. El-Reedy, who years later would become Ambassador to the UN for Egypt, was taken from his room and, still wearing his pyjamas, was forcibly put on a flight back to the United States.

Suddenly I'm Pregnant

On my return to Cuba I started to go out more often, dressed in my uniform so that I could blend in better and not attract attention. I spent most of my time trying to look beautiful so as to be ready for Fidel, something that I realise now could be unsettling, but I think it's understandable given how much I was in love. When I was in New York, Joe had commented that I was putting on weight and I soon found out it had nothing to do with my diet. In May 1959, I started to feel sick, particularly in the mornings, and I couldn't eat anything except lettuce or drink anything but milk and I vomited. Fidel joked with me, saying I should eat more rice and beans. However, for all his joking, I realised what had really happened: I was pregnant. When I told Fidel, his first reaction was to open his eyes wide and then he went very quiet. It was clear that I had caught him by surprise and initially he seemed at a loss but he accepted the situation. He didn't object at all and he tried to calm me.

'Everything is going to be all right,' he told me.

I was happy, so happy. I was going to have a baby! I wanted to go straight out and buy clothes, start preparing a room for the baby, and I began to dream about it, without considering what my parents would say because, although I worried about how they would react, what could they do about it? I didn't want to leave Fidel. It was his child as well and, anyway, I couldn't leave him. He said that all children of Cuban parentage belonged to Cuba.

A Dark Man

In May 1959 they transferred me without warning to the Hotel Riviera for a few days where I would meet someone who would be as important in my life as Fidel, although for different reasons. At that first meeting, I didn't find out his name. I just saw a man with dark hair who looked Italian and was dressed in a military uniform that I recognised was from Fidel's air force. Without

93

even telling me his name, he said:

'I know who you are. I know that you're Fidel's girlfriend. If you need help, I can give it to you. I can take you away from here. I'm American.'

I refused his offer, telling him that I wasn't looking for help and I didn't want to leave the island. I told Fidel who asked me to describe the man who had approached me and he became very angry when he heard what I had to say.

'Don't talk to him and stay away from him,' he replied sharply.

I found out later that his name was Frank Fiorini and that's how I knew him for many years until I saw him on television in June 1972, named as Frank Sturgis, one of the five people arrested when they took out some poorly installed microphones in the campaign offices of the Democratic Party in the Watergate Building, the first thread that led to the unravelling of the confusing tangle of corruption and illegal activities that would end up forcing Richard Nixon to resign from office. But this would be some time later. At that first meeting in Cuba in 1959, he was Frank Fiorini to me and that's how he was known by Fidel and his men as well. He had been co-operating with them since 1957.

Fiorini had been the messenger between the guerillas in the mountains and the hidden operatives of the 26th of July Movement in Havana and Santiago. He had traded arms and munitions from United States to the Sierra Maestra. He hadn't been a disinterested collaborator, though. Nor was he motivated by ideology or solidarity. He was part of a plot to win the confidence of Fidel and his men to obtain information for Carlos Prío, the former president who had been kicked out by the dictator Fulgencio Batista, during his *coup d'état* in 1952. Prío had been a progressive politician in his youth and abandoned his ideals as his personal fortune increased through very lucrative collaborations with corrupt Cuban politicians and also his agreement with Lucky Luciano and the Mafia, which not only controlled gambling but also drug trafficking on the island.

When Prío became President of Cuba in 1948, he spread the use of armed violence. First it was political then overtly criminal and it was known as *pistolerismo* [gun law]. After Batista's coup in 1952, he was exiled to the United States, to Florida, in fact, and that's where he met Fiorini.

As I would gradually discover, Fiorini never played for one side only. Once the revolution had succeeded, and having gained the friendship and confidence of Fidel, he broadened his alliances beyond Prío. He had an interview with an agent from the CIA in Havana and offered, voluntarily, to collaborate 'one hundred percent in providing information', an offer that wasn't rejected, according to official documents. The CIA sent a cable recommending 'they try to develop Fiorini', the language with which the CIA established that they were going to use him as an operative. He started to be seen frequently in the US Embassy with Erickson Nichols and Robert Van Horn, the air force attachés in the diplomatic legation. He was able to satisfy their demands which put him 'in a good position' to obtain intelligence when Pedro Díaz Lanz, chief of the Cuban air force, appointed him head of security and espionage. The CIA and FBI wanted all the information that Fiorini could also get on the advances and growth of communism in Cuba, on the potential infiltration of communists in the ranks of the Cuban army, of possible plans by the island to collaborate with other Caribbean and Latin American countries in their own revolutions and on possible internal movements against Fidel.

As if working for Prío and Washington

wasn't enough, there was another side for which the inscrutable, multifaceted Fiorini provided his service. I don't think it was by accident that I saw him the first time at the same place and time that I met Charles *Babe* Baron, an important figure in organised crime in Chicago and the associate of another key figure in the Mafia, Sam Giancana. In the eyes of a young girl like me with little experience, Baron was just an old man, a kind grandfather and a bit of a bootlegger. However, he was the general manager of the Riviera, a hotel that had opened in Havana in December 1957 and which had become, in a very short space of time, the main establishment for the Mafia outside of Las Vegas. The proprietor of the Riviera was Meyer Lansky, also known as *Little Man* because of his small stature. He was small but he was also one of the principal figures in the Kosher Nostra, the Jewish Mafia, which maintained alliances on the island with the Cosa Nostra, the Italian Mafia.

The Mafia in Cuba
Organised crime had started doing business in Cuba after the abolition of Prohibition in the United States and in 1933 Lansky signed an agreement with Batista to buy the

molasses on the island that 'the syndicate' needed to set itself up as an essential player in the buoyant alcohol production business. In that handshake in 1933, *Little Man* also agreed a plan to begin establishing and to set up an influential Mafia colony on the island. In exchange for a commission, Batista allowed Mafia-owned hotels and casinos to operate without police interference. With Santo Trafficante Jr., another important Mafia figure in the United States and Cuba, Lansky was one of the key people, when the organised crime empire returned, to increase their interests in the 1950s when Batista regained power, with the added goal of making Cuba the centre for heroin distribution in that part of the world. This was a stated objective recorded in a meeting one week in 1946 that the most important members of the different Mafia families, including Lucky Luciano, attended at the National Hotel in Havana under cover of a concert by a rising star: Frank Sinatra.

In those first moments after the triumph of the revolution, Fidel decreed that all casinos be closed but on 19 February, after the marked fall in tourism, he allowed them to reopen but imposed taxes on them that would be used to pay for social programmes.

Many things began to be very different under Fidel than they had been with Batista as well. Soon they started arresting the Mafia in Cuba.

Those arrests are one of the reasons why I believe that my first meeting at the Riviera with Fiorini was not mere chance. He had been in touch with and personally knew all the heavyweights in the Mafia like Joe Rivers, Charlie *The Blade* Tourine and Jake Lansky, the brother of *Little Man*. Soon he began doing favours for them, and that was what Baron was trying to get from me as he obviously knew that I was Castro's lover. In those few days at the hotel which had been arranged for me, he started to bombard me with requests, asking me if I would say this or that to Fidel or to deliver messages or letters to him. These requests continued when I returned to the Hilton where messages continued to reach me via one of their lawyers. They asked me to intercede on behalf of Lansky's younger brother who had been in charge of the casino at the National Hotel and was imprisoned in 'el Presidio Modelo' [the Model Prison] on Los Pinos Island. It was a brutal prison in Batista's time and it was where Fidel was sent after he was sentenced following the assault on the Moncada Barracks. Tired of answering their calls, I took one of the blank sheets of paper that Fidel had signed with a large F and, as Celia and Yáñez did, I filled it in with an order to release Lansky and a couple of other men from Los Pinos.

Wearing my honorary uniform, I went with Yáñez to the island with a black sand beach and mangoes where the prison was situated and where Fidel had coined the phrase 'history will absolve me', repeating the argument which he used when he was condemned and imprisoned by Batista. When I went in, I was horrified by what I saw; people were packed together like sardines. There was continuous shouting and the prisoners were like animals, livestock all of them. Yáñez identified the men whose names were in the document and I went up to them and said to them, one by one, 'you, let's go'. They hugged me and I felt proud, strong, important. I still felt that when Fidel found out what had happened. I tried to explain that holding these people in prison would work against him, that they didn't want to do him any harm and that perhaps he might need them in the future. But in any case, the explanations didn't matter because Fidel wasn't angry, or at least he indicated that it didn't matter so much. I think he even laughed that I had

had the audacity to put the names on an official document.

After that episode, I saw Fiorini several times. The second time was at the Habana Libre, the day when I went to the jeweller's to pick up a ring that Fidel had ordered for me which we had designed together with diamonds forming his initials, FC, and an inscription on the inside. I bumped into Frank who insisted that I go to the bar with him. He wrote on a napkin,

'I can help you.'

Yáñez was sitting behind me on a bench. I told Fiorini that I didn't need his help and that I didn't want anything and I also told him that Fidel had asked me to stay away from him. None of this stopped him approaching me and he not only offered me help I didn't need but also asked me to do him favours, including taking papers from Fidel's suite, whatever documents I could get. Stuck in my own world of a jealous woman in love, I told him that all the letters Fidel received were from female admirers. He insisted. I asked him why he needed me when, with his own 26th of July Movement uniform and his role in the air force, he could go to as many meetings as he wanted to. He justified it by saying that I had more access and I stayed in the room that had

101

the safe and the papers when everyone else had gone. He was so insistent that, to make him leave me in peace, I began to take documents that Fidel threw away after reading or left scattered round the room and I would give them to Fiorini, who was delighted, although I told him that what I was getting for him was material that was of no interest to Castro. Frank started to press me to speak to Fidel in favour of 'tourism', Fiorini's way of defending his friends' casinos. He wanted me to tell him, as well, about my lover's trips and movements. He was so annoying and so insistent that I agreed, through sheer boredom.

It might seem strange but I was tired of him and I thought that by giving him those papers or some information I would get rid of him once and for all. I was convinced that I wasn't giving him anything of value and I always took care to make sure there was nothing there that would harm Fidel. I also thought that if I collaborated with him in some way it might reach the ears of my mother, who I wrote to from time to time, so that she would know I was all right.

Condemned Not to Forget

My pregnancy was moving along. I had to stop wearing the uniform because it no longer fitted and the bigger I got the more I worried I became. Although I told myself 'I'm a woman, I can do it', someone — and I have never known who — was about to stand in my way and leave me with an enormous and distressing hole in my life which I have never been able to fill.

I don't remember the exact date when the nightmare began but I know it was autumn. Fidel was on a trip, to Oriente Province I think, and I was at the hotel where I had breakfast in the room as usual. I drank a glass of milk and soon afterwards I felt groggy and lost consciousness. I heard voices. I have vague memories of hearing a siren and of lying on a stretcher with a drip and I remember that I heard a cry, like a mewing kitten . . .

I have never known exactly what happened. Who ordered this savage attack? Was it Fidel's men? Was it the CIA? According to some versions, I was subjected to an abortion. According to others, birth was induced and the baby was stolen from me. They say the operation, whatever it was, was conducted by a doctor called Ferrer who wasn't even a gynaecologist but a heart surgeon. They also say that Fidel ordered him to be shot when he found out what had happened. Unfortunately, I can't confirm anything. I would have liked to have been awake and not drugged, as extreme as that might seem, to know exactly what happened.

I don't know how much time passed before I woke up in the Havana Hilton again but I wasn't in the suite I had shared with Fidel but in a more modest, dark room, lying on the bed in terrible pain, feeling sick and thirsty. I didn't care what they had done to me. I was bleeding, dying and I would have died there if Camilo Cienfuegos hadn't appeared just then.

'Oh my God — fuck! Baby, what happened to you?' he exclaimed when he discovered me there in that state.

He got me some medication straight away, called my brother Joe, who was furious, and organised everything so that I could leave there immediately. I knew that I had to go if I wanted to survive. I needed medical attention to stop the haemorrhaging and the pain and I didn't know any doctors in Cuba. After what had happened, I didn't trust anyone either. There were still a lot of people loyal to Batista and I didn't know who was who. It was time to go home. Otherwise, if I stayed there and died, my death would be used against Fidel. If I was sure about anything, it was that he wasn't behind what had happened to me. Fidel would never have done anything like that.

Cienfuegos helped me to dress because I couldn't do it on my own. He took me down to the street where a jeep picked us up and took me to the airport. Once there, I embarked on a Cuban Airlines flight to the United States. Some days later, on 28 October 1959, the Cessna light aircraft on which Camilo was travelling to Havana from Camagüey, where they had arrested his friend Huber Matos, who was accused of treason by Fidel, disappeared with him on board. His mysterious disappearance has never been resolved. He saved my life and to this day I love him for that.

CHAPTER 3
AN IMPOSSIBLE MISSION: KILL CASTRO

After all I have lived through and suffered in Cuba, the first few days back in New York were horrible. I had lost everything; I didn't even have Fidel and I thought my baby was dead. An agonising doubt about what had really happened was the only thing that gave me a tiny bit of hope, small as it was. I was tired and confused and most of the time, as in Bergen-Belsen, crying was the only thing I had the energy for. I didn't trust anyone and I couldn't see a way out. Some people said that my baby was alive, some assured me my baby was dead, while others suggested that Fidel had killed my child. I just wanted silence. So I decided to say nothing.

My beloved brother Joe, who had been working at the United Nations and hoped to complete a doctorate in international relations, had left for Argentina on a Fulbright scholarship. Philip, who was studying for a degree in New York under the tutelage of the highly regarded Chilean maestro Claudio Arrau, was becoming a renowned concert pianist and was frequently away on tour. Valerie, who at sixteen had decided to live with relatives rather than move around with the family, had married Robert C. Paul, a distributor for Budweiser beer, and had moved to Harrisburg, Pennsylvania. All I had was mama who returned from a mission for the army in Heidelberg to be with me. But we argued all the time. In spite of our love for each other in those early days after my return my only memories of her are constant arguments.

Hatred, Fear and Loneliness
FBI agents came to our apartment and took turns in keeping me under surveillance. They questioned me about the time I spent in Cuba and I had the feeling that they were looking at me with contempt, as if they were silently asking me how I could have had an intimate relationship with 'that communist'. Their antipathy hurt but much worse was the feeling that mama thought the same as them or was one of them. I felt the same fear and loneliness that I had suffered as a child in the hospital in Drangstedt and I just wanted to sleep, not think and not feel. On top of that, I was going mad with the

drugs they were giving me, a combination of drugs that gave me euphoric highs and desperate lows. I was riding a roller coaster of emotions that prevented any kind of mental stability. After sleeping through the day, I woke up at night disorientated and miserable, feeling that I was wasting my time and my life. I reached the point where I hated everyone. I was broken up inside and at the same time filled with hate. I wanted to go back to Cuba and kill whoever had killed my child — or whoever had torn my baby out of me.

Several agents came to the house but the ones assigned to me were FBI agents Frank Lundquist and Frank O'Brien, whose almost constant presence in the apartment made them seem like part of the furniture. Without a shadow of a doubt their looks betrayed them as members of Edgar Hoover's Bureau, with their suits and ties and their perfect hair. With their extreme courtesy and good manners they developed an almost paternal relationship with me, gradually winning my confidence. They started taking me to their office at the FBI, the head office of the Federal Agency in New York at 221 East 69th Street. I was turning into a robot and I tried to be good and obedient. But behind the façade of kindness shown by Frank & Frank, as I always called them, I could clearly identify other intentions.

From the beginning I knew that they were trying to educate me in their way of thinking, brainwashing me and taking advantage of my emotional fragility at that time. They talked incessantly about the evils of communism and how important it was to destroy it to save Americans. They didn't stop being rude about Fidel and even told me quite openly that we had to do something so that the world would see him in a bad light. They had no qualms about going for the emotional jugular either in their attempts to convert me to the cause against 'the red menace' which had become a major nightmare for the United States, and turn me against Fidel. They put me under tremendous psychological pressure with photographs of my allegedly aborted baby and so-called medical documents which confirmed that the operation had left me sterile. They were also giving me tablets which were supposed to be vitamins but I am convinced, although I can't prove it, that they were something else altogether.

Mama went to the 69th Street offices of the FBI quite frequently at this time. She introduced me to Alex Rorke in the days after my return; he was a Jesuit from a very good family with close links to the Kennedys. The son of a district attorney in the District of Manhattan and alumnus of the School of Foreign Service at Georgetown University, Rorke had served in the Second World War as a specialist in military espionage for the US Army, where they must have met; he also worked freelance for the press and was always armed with a camera and with mama, who had also worked at *Stars and Stripes,* a military publication. He was a collaborator with the FBI and the CIA; attractive, elegant, it was as if he had just stepped out of one of the offices in Madison Avenue. Alex became a kind of big brother to me and we spent a lot of time together having long conversations and visiting the churches he attended, including St Patrick's Cathedral. Mama's family had been Quakers and *papa*'s Protestant but I hadn't been brought up in any particular religion so Alex found virgin territory in me, teaching me Catholic rituals and prayers in an attempt to convert me.

Rorke and the FBI were pushing me to get involved in different groups which, in those days, represented both sides of the struggle in the United States: those in favour of and those against Fidel and the revolution. I began to meet Cubans who would become key individuals in secret activities organised in exile against Fidel, such as Manuel Artime, who had founded the Movimiento de Recuperación Revolucionaria [Movement for Revolutionary Recovery] and had just escaped from Cuba. I also met Rolando Masferrer, *El Tigre* [The Tiger], a tall, powerfully built man, very macho, very Cuban, who had won support during Batista's dictatorship for his role leading the savage private army that brutally terrorised civilians who opposed the regime. Masferrer was such a controversial figure that the ambassador, Philip Bonsal [US Ambassador to Cuba], had placed him at the top of a list of dangerous persons in an advisory report for the Eisenhower administration on negative reactions that might be received by giving asylum in the United States to close to three hundred supporters of Batista that Cuba described as 'war criminals'.

I met Artime, Masferrer and others like them at meetings that Rorke took me to for groups such as the International Anti-Communist Brigade where they used me for propaganda, creating an interesting version of my case, painting Fidel as a monster to help them fundraise to finance their activities. They hired school halls and local buildings for these meetings, where they showed films, played music and gave speeches in which Artime, already a loud individual, went mad, bordering on hysteria, when he jeered and insulted Fidel. I remember extremely well his contorted face as he laid furiously into Fidel: 'Communist! Communist!' He looked like an irrational lunatic which of course delighted the anti-Castro supporters and brought in more donations.

'Welcome On Board'

I met Frank Nelson at one of these meetings, a suspicious character involved with the Mafia in Ohio. He lived at 240 Central Park South, a luxurious apartment lit by red lights like a Chinese bordello, and it was another of the meeting places where they planned activities against Castro. Nelson was also in charge of Frank Fiorini's finances and I met Fiorini again in that apartment for the first time since leaving Cuba. The day I met Frank again he greeted me with 'congratulations, welcome on board'. He told me that he was sorry about what had happened to me and promised that they would compensate me. Then he started talking enthusiastically about the plans to overthrow Fidel, stating proudly

112

that they had 'an army' to carry them out.

Alongside the anti-Castro meetings, I also assisted at meetings for the 26th of July Movement where I got my membership card and became 'propaganda secretary, H branch'. I went to approximately twenty of those pro-Castro and pro-revolutionary meetings which were held in places like the Belvedere Hotel on 48th Street or the Casa Cuba club on Columbus Avenue and also at La Barraca, a restaurant in mid-town Manhattan that I loved. They shared and discussed the latest news about what was happening on the island and in exile and also in American, Latin American and world politics. They organised information and propaganda campaigns as well which were financed by contributions from members and with our seventy-five cents contribution per week it could be assumed that we were also helping to raise funds so that Fidel could buy military equipment. They were meetings with music and fabulous food and people I liked, such as Olga Blanca. I had met her on one of the crossings on the *Berlin* where we had our photograph taken together with my mother and *papa* in the captain's cabin. Personally, I felt much happier in those meetings with Cubans who stood up for the revolution and for Fidel than when I was with people like Fiorini, Nelson, Artime or Masferrer, but my presence there was also a question of work. For instance, I went to La Barraca with Yáñez Pelletier on a trip he made to New York on 19 December 1959, a meeting which, as with everything that happened in that group, I dutifully reported to the FBI agents. I also informed them when Yáñez called me and said he was thinking about defecting.

Those weren't easy times and eventually I had to distance myself from certain people. In those days, no one trusted anyone and everyone suspected everyone else and I was no exception. This hurt because to be with the Cubans was a way of staying in contact with Cuba, fostering the hope that it wouldn't be impossible to return, and I had promised myself I would return. Olga Blanca was one of the women who came to these meetings. I had met her from time to time and was even photographed with her in *papa*'s cabin when he docked with the *Berlin* in New York. She encouraged me to return saying things like 'the King is waiting for you'. However, I knew that this wasn't the moment. If I did try to, I was convinced that the Americans would lock me up or punish my mother.

At the end of 1959, when I was living at my parents' apartment, I received a telegram from Cuba telling me that I should call a number on the island. I didn't know who was behind the request, nor what it could be about, but I was still tormented by the loss of my child and I needed to talk to someone, anyone, who might have some answers. Convinced that the telephone at home was bugged, I took advantage of a moment when the agents who were watching me had gone and I left the house to call from a phone box in the next street, Riverside Drive. While I was on the telephone, a couple of gunshots broke the window. Terrified and with cuts from the broken glass, I went home as quickly as I could. The agents, who had by now returned, came running towards me, immediately saying that Fidel's men had been responsible. I never really knew if that was the case or not but, as with so many incidents in those days, I couldn't prove that it wasn't, nor could I identify who was responsible with any certainty. Had it really been Cubans? Why? Was it another FBI plot to turn me against Fidel? There were more questions than answers and the only thing I was certain about was that I was in somebody's sights.

I was an obvious inconvenience for someone. In my emotional state, I was also easily manipulated. More than anything, I was useful and my value as an activist was beginning to become clear in the growing number of plans to get rid of Fidel which came from the anti-Castro exiles, the Mafiosi who had seen their lucrative business deals in Havana closed down and the government of the United States, sometimes acting separately and sometimes together. They had a few people available to them with such personal access to Fidel and getting close to him was a fundamental part of more than one of these sinister plots.

The only thing left to do was to confirm that, in spite of my dramatic departure from the island, I still had unlimited access. So Frank decided to send me to Cuba in December 1959 to see if I could still move around freely in the circles closest to Fidel and get to Fidel himself. He organised a very short incursion, a test mission really, and I flew there and back on the same day with neither time nor strength to think or feel. The only thing I learned from that trip was that my key for the Habana Libre still opened the door to room 2408. I also took back with me to the United States some letters from admirers and documents and maps. I imagine their value was minimal but they at least showed that I had been inside Fidel's suite.

The trip was organised very rapidly. It had to happen in December because a propaganda campaign about my experiences in Cuba was about to commence and it would not reflect well on my lover in Havana. On 1 January 1960 my parents wrote an open letter to Fidel in which they stated that if he had 'any sense of justice, honour or moral character' he would compensate me for the loss of my 'honour and name' and cover the costs of my medical and psychological treatment after the operation in which I lost my child. Since my return from Cuba, I had had to go to the Roosevelt Hospital in New York several times because I was haemorrhaging frequently. Closing their letter, they created a play on words of one of Fidel's emblematic phrases: 'Let history absolve you . . . if it can'. They sent copies to presidents, ambassadors and dignitaries in the United States, Germany and Cuba, as well as several media networks, senators, the FBI and even the Pope. I was furious when I found out about it but I should have saved my anger for later: that damned letter was only an aperitif for what was yet to come.

Shortly afterwards, my beloved Alex Rorke

was the brains behind another chapter in the campaign of slander launched by the American authorities against Fidel. They used me like a marionette, a physically and emotionally broken puppet that was easy to manipulate in whatever way they wanted. Alex came up with the idea of an article that appeared in *Confidential,* a quarterly tabloid specialising in scandals about celebrities and politicians that had revealed, for example, that Bing Crosby abused his wife and that the actor Rock Hudson and the musician Liberace were homosexual. As *Newsweek* put it on one occasion, *Confidential* offered 'sin and sex with a sprinkling of right-wing politics'. With several million readers despite its shameless sensationalism, its success was undeniable and as Humphrey Bogart once said, 'everyone reads it but says it was the cook who brought it into the house'. The fake story of my adventures in Cuba that was published in those pages was perfect for a publication like that, and its huge audience ideal for enabling it to succeed in its objective to smear Fidel and foster hatred.

Lies and Propaganda

The article in question, in which my mother had so willingly collaborated, written from her personal point of view, was entitled 'Castro raped my teen-age daughter' and it was a crude pack of lies. According to the article, Fidel had deceived me and taken me to Cuba. He had held me prisoner, raped me, robbing me of my virginity, and had held me kidnapped and drugged to use me like a sex toy. That infamous text also said that when I found myself pregnant, Fidel was angry and his people started to give me drugs to try to cause me to abort the baby. It told how one day I tried to escape and that Yáñez Pelletier had attacked me, kicking me in the stomach to try, unsuccessfully, to make me lose the baby. It also explained how, finally, a Dr Ferrer was forced at gunpoint by Yáñez to carry out a bungled abortion, as they described it, 'under the direct orders of Fidel Castro'. After the operation, the doctor was killed. Fidel was portrayed as a cruel murderer who executed people in the street and the article attributed apparently verbatim quotes to him such as 'in a dictatorship, the Church has to go', something that I never heard him say and in which I could clearly see Alex's hand, so anti-communist and so Catholic.

When the article was published I argued a lot with my mother.

'This propaganda shit doesn't work,' I protested.

'Peaches,' mama replied very calmly, 'you're angry. He's no good. You'll forget him.'

She was wrong. How could I forget? Fidel, Cuba, my child and all that had happened was still in my head and my life and everything was going really badly for me. My heart was broken, I had no hope and I felt that no one cared at all. No one wanted to talk about the truth or give me the help I needed. I was just a pawn in biased games of propaganda-filled political chess. Although I had mama, I felt so alone that I decided to go to Germany, to return to my rock and seek refuge in *papa*.

At our reunion I cried a lot, eaten up by the sense that I had disappointed him or shamed him and I promised that I would make him proud of me. However, I soon realised that he didn't want to talk about what had happened.

'It's OK, don't worry. You made a mistake, that's all. You have to get over it and learn from it,' he said to me, trying to calm me down and refusing to discuss anything further.

Papa seemed happy to have me in his house, Am Leher Tor 1C in Bremerhaven. I wanted to stay, learn to cook and work at Uncle Fritz's hotel to learn about the catering business. I wanted to take steps toward a normal, quiet life although the haemorrhaging that forced me to go to hospital several times was a painful reminder of what had happened.

I had no intention of leaving Germany but then that damned *Confidential* article crossed the ocean and appeared in the German press. This put an end to my tranquillity and anonymity and now I started to receive nasty looks, comments and insults, even threats, from the neighbours. Alex Rorke was writing to me daily as well, keeping me in touch with everything that was going on and his letters captivated me. He asked me if I would go back and in September 1960 that's what I did. I went back.

In the Everglades

After my return from Germany to the United States, I began participating in activities which were clearly illegal. I remember perfectly the first trip I made to Miami, a gun-running operation which meant travelling by car as part of a convoy that went through Georgia. During the trip, with the trunks full of guns, we picked up people along the way. Mama knew then that

I was getting involved in something that was too dark even for her, despite being so used to this shady world, and she didn't want me to go. But she gave in and let me go because Alex, whom she trusted completely, was involved in the operation and would be travelling on that same convoy. There were also at least a couple of other people who were going with us and they were taking drugs to keep themselves awake.

When the journey ended and we reached Miami, we stayed in a room in a three- or four-storey building, one of those cheap hotels typical of Florida and painted pink, purple or blue. This was where the soldiers who were preparing for the invasion of Cuba to overthrow Fidel lived. It was an old building close to some factories and the people there were mostly young and wearing military and camouflage clothing. There were also soldiers of fortune there, mercenaries and people with obvious military training. Although the majority were Cubans, there was quite a mixture. I remember, for example, that I met at least a couple of Hungarian 'freedom fighters' at this hotel, who were very dedicated, vicious, evil and well trained and older than almost all the other sons of Cuban landowners who were, on average, about twenty years old.

I met Fiorini again and, whether I wanted to or not, I became totally involved in the operation whose objective was to remove Fidel from power. In that respect I assumed that Frank was one of the people in charge of the assassination group in particular. He himself confirmed that and he assured me that the operation was financed with money from the CIA. This was about the so-called Operation 40, a classified government plot that Eisenhower had approved in March 1960. At the head of it were Vice-President Nixon and Allen Dulles, then the director of the CIA. The directive from the National Security Council that the President signed, which was kept secret for years, authorised the Agency to train and equip Cuban refugees as a guerrilla force to overthrow Fidel's government.

Years later, Fiorini explained publically how it worked: on one side, they integrated lots of CIA operatives, including double agents in Cuban intelligence, whose principal task was to train people to infiltrate a foreign country and establish contact with members of underground movements, the government and the armed forces of the country. On the other side, there was a second group which Frank called 'the assassination group', which he admitted being a part of and in which I worked alongside him. It was a command ready to act when it received orders to execute politicians or members of the armed forces. This included, if necessary, executing members of the group itself suspected of being double agents who were not working for the United States but for the country they claimed to infiltrate. Fiorini spoke in the plural, of countries, but at the time I realised that there was only one nation they had in mind, one single focus of attention: Cuba.

In my first few days in Miami I spent the majority of the time in the motel which became an operations headquarters. Occasionally I spent time at the house of an executive of the Cobbs Fruit Company, Irwin Charles Cardin. Alex Rorke had introduced me to him and he had a daughter about my age, Robin. Cardin wasn't a soldier of fortune like others who were all over Florida at the time; he was a wealthy man who wanted to be one of the chiefs and to be involved in the organisational and financial sides, not just the attacks on Fidel but, more than that, the plans for the island afterwards, if it succeeded in bringing down the revolutionary regime, and installing someone more favourable to the interests of American business again. On other occasions, I went to the training camps in the Everglades, the wetlands in the south of Florida full of snakes and mosquitoes that the mercenaries and youngsters lived with and where, with the support of exiles like Artime and the American government, they planned to overthrow Fidel in what would ultimately become the failed invasion of the Bay of Pigs.

We took advantage of the trips to Miami to transport arms. In the training camps in the Everglades there were people like Gerry Patrick Hemming, a serviceman for the CIA who, like Fiorini, had also collaborated with the 26th of July Movement and Fidel when they attacked the Batista regime in Sierra Maestra. In his day on the Cuban side, he had flown missions against American planes that tried to destroy sugar plantations, one of the main sources of income for the island. Like Frank, it hadn't taken Hemming long to turn against the Cuban revolution soon after its triumph but I think that, in his case, he did it because he was fervently anti-communist, not because of the influences of the various shadier alliances that drove Fiorini. It would explain why he would later resign as a commander in INTERPEN, the acronym for a group known as the Intercontinental Penetration Force, a bogus organisation that would provide cover for the US government to hide behind and negotiate connections with operations against Cuba from Florida and Guatemala. But that would come later. When I met him, he took part in Operation 40 as a military adviser.

Hemming was attractive and well-built. He spoke a bit of German because in the Second World War he was stationed in Germany as a specialist in sabotage. In the Everglades that was one of the key elements in the training camps, where we were taught military tactics which replicated the modus operandi of an army with instructors, discipline and classes. Hemming was very tall and always wore combat boots and an Australian hat. He gave classes on survival techniques, shooting with different arms such as rifles, M-1s, automatic weapons, pistols and bayonets and he even taught us how to throw knives. He liked to show off by claiming he could make anything fly through the air.

I changed in this environment, little by little, without wanting to or, at least, without doing so consciously. I still felt more lost than ever, and I found it impossible to know if I was good or bad. Perhaps everyone was good *and* bad, and that clear distinctions are impossible to make, probably not a good idea and almost always wrong in a world where disinformation and two or even three sides to a situation are part of the rules of the game. What I was certain about was that this was the most stupid and non-secret 'invisible army' ever invented where every other word was 'invasion', 'kill the bastard' or 'kill Fidel'.

There was one particular moment when I didn't think I fitted in there. I told Frank I was leaving but he refused to accept this and replied that I didn't fit in where I was going either. I was very important to them and I had been trained.

'Each one of us,' he explained, 'has a job to do.'

Objective: To Change History

In a world where everybody had a job to do, as Fiorini had said, I didn't know which one belonged to me. He started to make it clear a little while later when, at the end of 1960 or the beginning of 1961, I took a trip to New York with Alex Rorke to see my mother and Frank & Frank, O'Brien and Lundquist. In that visit to Manhattan, they spoke to me about killing Fidel for the first time, although the expression they used was a gentler, but no less lethal 'it would be good to neutralise him'.

127

The message was brutal, although as well as dressing it up in words that masked its harshness Alex mixed it all up with his Catholic ideology. That conversation in which I heard about my mission for the first time took place in the FBI building on 69th Street, not in an office but in a corridor because Rorke was afraid of being bugged. Afterwards, little by little, the logistics of it were revealed to me: we would use pills, a method they said would be 'suitable for a woman'. I would only have to put the contents of the pills into Fidel's food or drink and leave. He wasn't going to suffer too much and, supposedly, neither would I.

Once I had absorbed what I had heard and what it meant, I turned to Alex:

'You're asking me to kill him,' I said.

'Sometimes God works in ways that we don't understand,' he replied. 'It's his will. He will absolve you. You'll do it in the name of God and country.'

'Why do I have to do it, Alex?' I asked, still finding it hard to believe.

'He ruined your life,' he reminded me.

'I'm not going to kill him. I can't take someone else's life.'

I thought the whole thing was absurd, illogical, mad, incredible and ridiculous, and I still think so, but what I thought didn't matter. They left it with Rorke to try to convince me, so he and I had a second conversation then a third, then a fourth. Then he started mixing his message of a divine mission with something more earthly like money, showing me the motto on US dollar bills, 'In God we trust', giving me to understand that if I carried out the mission he was entrusting to me, I would never have to worry about money again and my life would always be secure, at least financially.

I don't know how many meetings there were, I would say about twenty, with O'Brien and Lundquist, with CIA agents, in the FBI offices and in my house. Finally, I agreed to it. In reality, I think that with all the 'vitamins' they were still giving me I would have agreed to anything. In any case, some poison that supposedly would cause a painless death seemed, without doubt, a kinder method than shooting Fidel or sticking a knife into his body, the one I knew so well and which had given me so much pleasure.

There was no shortage of options on how to get at the man I had been hopelessly in love with. Secret CIA plans to finish off Fidel were already in train as early as 1959. It included preposterous ideas such as giving him hallucinogenic drugs so that he would lose control and present a pathetic image which would destroy his charismatic leadership; contaminating the air in the radio station where he delivered speeches with a substance similar to LSD so that he would lose coherence; injecting one of his cigars with some chemical substance that would affect his reasoning and even make him lose his iconic beard by putting toxic thallium salts in his boots. What was being planned in my case was way beyond that: it was, in effect, murder.

What they told me was that the pills I had to put in Fidel's food or drink had been 'specially made in Chicago' and a man called Johnny Rosselli was going to supply them to me. It's likely that I may have come across him in Cuba without realising it as Rosselli was the manager at the San Souci, another iconic club in Havana, and one of the key men on the island for Sam Giancana, the godfather of the Chicago Mafia.

In any case, I knew Rosselli personally and, without a doubt, I met him in Miami when Frank Fiorini — it was always Frank — introduced me to this attractive man with a penetrating gaze. He was always elegantly dressed and they called him Mr Hollywood. The introduction took place at a meeting in the Fontainebleau, a hotel in Miami, and the person in control at that meeting was Robert Maheu, a man who had represented the interests of millionaire Howard Hughes in Washington whose aviation business had signed secret contracts with the CIA and the Department of Defence. Maheu had been recruited by the CIA's Office for National Security in 1954 and he had good relationships with the Mafia and he had negotiated with Rosselli on other occasions. He had problems with the IRS which led him to seek alliances with people in power. For September 1960, Maheu organised a meeting in the Plaza in New York between Jim O'Connell, a high ranking official at the Department for Security, and Rosselli where they started to develop plans for the assassination. Back then, the CIA laboratories had already stepped up the pace and were experimenting with different ways of getting rid of Fidel, among which included the use of the botulism toxin, the most lethal known.

It was a few months after that decisive meeting at the Plaza in New York that I had my meeting with Maheu and Rosselli in the Fontainebleau in Miami, a meeting in which Frank Fiorini, Alex Rorke and a couple of other men I couldn't identify also participated. I remember hearing them talking in low voices about me, about what had happened with my baby, about how this would be my revenge. They discussed the plans more openly among themselves. With a billing as a spiteful lover who would be the perfect assassin, I felt stupid, important and frightened all at the same time and also cornered, thinking that I couldn't say no in front of all these people. So I drew on all my strength and tried to say:

'I don't know if I can do it.'

'You'll do it for your country,' replied Frank brusquely.

'What happens if I fail?'

'You won't fail.'

Then he opened a box, inside which was a packet containing the two pills, and announced:

'This is going to change history.'

'Don't Do It'

That night I went back to the 'guerrilla' hotel and tried to sleep, without much success, trying to ignore the fact that I had those two lethal pills but unable to prevent myself feeling extremely remorseful. What had happened? How was it possible that I was in this situation? Two years earlier I had been just a teenager whose rebelliousness had amounted to nothing more than avoiding authority, not doing what my parents asked me to do and from time to time sneaking on to the ships that *papa* captained as a stowaway. Now, two years on, I was a young woman who had fallen madly in love at first sight with a tall, bearded man with a handsome face, a great deal of charisma and an intense look, and I had given him my love, madly and passionately, without thinking about anything else. Now everything was different. I had become a woman suddenly and painfully and I had paid a high price: I had lost my child. I moved among special agents, secret operatives, exiles, business people, Mafiosi and mercenaries and they had given me the weapons to turn me into an assassin, the author of an assassination which would not only have marked me for life but would have marked history itself.

After an anxious night, Alex and Frank came to get me and I was ready with my Pan Am Airways bag and a small white make-up case, frightened to death but not wanting to show it. They took me to Miami airport but, just as I was about to board, Alex came up to me and, speaking in a very low voice almost without moving his lips so that Fiorini couldn't see or hear him, said:

'Don't do it.'

'Don't do it.' Three words from the mouth of the same man from whom I had first heard the proposal to 'neutralise' Fidel. *'Don't do it.'* A request? Advice? A warning? Anyway, the phrase made me see that I wasn't the only one tortured by guilt and I thought that perhaps poor Alex was assailed by moral doubts. It was also possible that, at the airport, he may have switched on his paternal conscience again, the one he had employed so often with me since we had met; perhaps he was alerting me as best he could to the fact that it couldn't be as easy as they had said it would be and there were plans to get rid of me or incriminate me if I was successful in executing the mission. A change of opinion or compassion, it didn't matter anyway. Alex's 'don't do it' didn't change anything because I had already made a decision and I knew that I wasn't going to kill Fidel: I didn't feel that I could.

The Reunion
My determination not to assassinate Fidel didn't prevent me being a bag of nerves on the flight. Unlike the quick day trip which had been organised by Fiorini in December 1959 to prove that this much more significant one could take place, this time my mission wasn't a test run and I embarked on it

134

with very different feelings. I knew that the open letter by my parents, the article in *Confidential* and all the publicity about my case had embarrassed me. Not only had they caused me to distance myself from the 26th of July Movement in New York but they hadn't reflected well on Fidel either. What's more, on the flight between Havana and Miami I worried that I would be searched on arrival in Cuba and the pills be discovered, so I decided to take them out of the trouser pocket I was carrying them in and put them into a jar of Pond's face cream.

The fear of being searched proved, shortly after, to be unfounded and when I landed there was no search of my luggage nor questioning at the airport so, without further delay, I went to my first stop, the Hotel Colina. I changed my clothes and, dressed once more in my honorary uniform, I went from there to the Habana Libre. I was a real bag of nerves but I managed not to show it, waved at everyone in the lobby and went up in the lift; I got to the twenty-fourth floor, headed for the bedroom and used the key in the door once again. I opened it, walked in and saw that Fidel wasn't there. Then I took out the jar of face cream from the make-up case and, taking the lid off, I saw that the pills had almost disintegrated and changed into a kind of paste. They were ruined and as I hadn't any intention of using them anyway it seemed much safer to me to throw them in the bidet. They took a while to go down the drain and I had to try several times but at last I saw them disappear and, when I was sure they had gone, I relaxed and breathed more easily. Above all, I felt free.

Not long afterwards, Fidel came to the room and I was very happy to see him although he seemed distant and as pre-occupied as ever.

'Oh! Alemanita,' he exclaimed when he saw me.

An 'I miss you' came out of my mouth, the first thing I could think of to say.

'Where have you been? With those people in Miami, the counter-revolutionaries?' he then asked. I know he didn't really expect a reply and he let out a long sigh which I could tell meant 'don't answer, I already know'. Then he sat down on the bed, took off his muddy boots and lay back. The ashtray was full of cigar butts, those Romeo y Julieta ones that were made especially for him, with his portrait and the date of the liberation on the band.

'I have to ask you what happened to me

136

on the day of the operation, about what happened to our child. That's the main reason I'm here,' I said.

'Not to kill me?' he replied.

As he always did with everyone, Fidel spoke to me looking me straight in the eye and I had no option but to tell the truth.

'Yes.'

Then he took his gun out of its holster, put it in his lap first then gave it to me. I picked it up, looked at it then looked at him as he continued to lay stretched out. He close his eyes and said,

'No one can kill me. No one. Ever.'

'I can,' I retorted.

'You won't do it,' he concluded.

He was right: I wasn't going to do it; I didn't want to do him any harm and would never have wanted to because, no matter how much I might have tried to convince myself to do it, I had to hate him enough to want to kill him. I dropped the gun and suddenly felt a great sense of liberation.

I started to cry. Fidel saw this and told me to come to the bed. I knelt there beside him and, unable to stop crying, in a hysterical state, I started shouting, demanding answers about our child. I hit the bed and even hit him and threw myself at him; he remained very calm and very softly tried to

137

pacify me.

'Everything's all right, everything's all right.'

'No,' I replied, dissatisfied. 'What happened?'

'I fixed everything. The doctor is dead.'

'But I don't know what happened,' I protested.

'I know, I know.'

'How do you know?'

'I know everything. It's not a problem. The boy is all right.'

'The boy is all right.' My son was alive! I wanted to see him, to cuddle him, and I started to try to persuade Fidel but he refused, cutting me short with a 'he's in good hands'. He told me that he was in the care of the Fernández family, the teachers I had visited several times. I wanted to run to their house, but I knew that it was impossible because my time on the island was limited. They were waiting in Miami for me to come back with the assassination mission completed and I was sure that CIA personnel were watching my every move on the island. Fidel also said that his son was 'a son of Cuba now'.

'He's mine as well,' I replied.

Then I started to threaten that I would come back with *papa* to get him back and he didn't like that at all, but in spite of my fury he was always kind to me. I lay down beside him and we started caressing and being attentive towards each other. He tried to sleep and wanted to rest because that evening he had to deliver a speech about racism and hatred but I had so many questions to ask. Like the adolescent in love that I was, reckless and jealous, I finally asked him if he was cheating on me and he replied, laughing:

'What do you want me to do here on my own? You are still my little German girl.'

After a while, he got from the bed, went to the bathroom to wash his face, put on clean boots, said that he had to go and gave me a big hug. I replied that I had to go as well and Fidel asked me not to, that I should stay, but we both knew that was impossible. It was a sad parting. Neither of us gained anything.

Alone in the room again, I reflected that if there was anything I didn't have the right to do it was to take someone's life for any reason — least of all for politics which I also didn't give a damn about. I think Fidel knew perfectly well how they had confused me and tried to use me. I told myself that I wanted to live and I would try to do so again, but despite the clarity with which I understood it all at the moment, I was also confused. I loved Fidel and longed to stay, but I had to go. What was I going to do with the $6,000 they had given me in case I needed to bribe anyone, hide or leave in a hurry? Should I stay and fight for my son, talk to Celia or someone else in Fidel's circle to try to find him? I believed that if I didn't go back to the United States as planned, they would come looking for me. If I went back, what were they going to say? How was I going to get out of this? I felt exhausted, worrying about how I was going to explain to Fiorini that I hadn't completed the mission and I felt a terrible wave of fear wash over me. It was a sensation that is difficult to put into words but it was as if I was at the centre of a hurricane and I couldn't escape. I was frightened to go back.

With tears in my eyes, I left the $6,000 with a note asking Fidel to invest the money for our son. I took some of the cigar bands as a memento and my make-up case, then left the room and went downstairs. After waving at those on reception again, I noticed a man by the shop holding a newspaper, and I had a feeling he was an American agent, more so when he nodded at me as if in greeting. I waved back. He probably thought I had killed Fidel — I was crying as

I left, full of emotion.

I went to the Hotel Colina to change, then to the airport and boarded the plane, as planned, which took off for Miami at six that evening.

Proud to Have Failed Them

I landed after a brief flight, tired, depressed and mentally exhausted, but I didn't have time to reflect or any time to myself. As soon as they opened the door of the plane, I saw Fiorini, Rorke and a dozen other men, some in military uniform, others in civilian clothing, and their anxiety was evident; they surrounded me and I was too frightened even to speak.

'OK, so how did it go?' I heard them ask me.

'I didn't do it,' I managed to say.

They couldn't believe it; they started to swear and yell insults at me and I saw Frank's eyes fire up with anger, as he grabbed me, took me to a van and threw me in the back where I started to babble excuses.

'I told you that Fidel doesn't have a fixed schedule so you never know when he's going to eat or drink or come and go. It's unpredictable.'

The more I talked, the angrier they became. When Alex started to argue with Frank trying to defend me, I excused myself saying something like: 'God didn't want it to turn out like that', an argument that annoyed the already irritated Frank even more.

He continued to feel suspicious while they transferred me to a safe house on the outskirts of the city, a concrete structure with no windows and a couple of bunks where Frank told me to wait. They must have switched on the radio somewhere else and listened to Fidel giving his lecture. If I had poisoned him with the two tablets, that wouldn't have happened so they had confirmation that the mission had failed.

From then on, I had to live with that 'failure' and, in truth, I have never been able to put it behind me. Even today, they still say that I'm notorious for having failed not only in one of the first attempts to kill Fidel but the one that had most chance of success. That's the view that one could have from the outside. But I am proud of myself, very proud, and I'm happy to have succeeded in consigning to hell all the brainwashing they submitted me to. I'm happy not to have taken all the pills they wanted me to take to alter my mind before going to Havana, make me go mad or start a fight with Fidel, drugs that would have put me in a state in which it would have been easy to find an excuse to have killed him.

Fidel knows exactly what happened that day and I think that secretly he must still be laughing. If I had been another person, perhaps I would have succeeded; you never know. I simply couldn't do it. It wasn't impossible for me to have done it. But I didn't.

CHAPTER 4
PÉREZ JIMÉNEZ:
MY SECOND DICTATOR

In room 2408 of the Habana Libre hotel I had taken the helm of a large ship and succeeded in maintaining the course of history. The contents of two pills would not change this course, although I had paid a high price and had to leave my child behind. I thought that I could go back and try to get him and that my parents would help me to apply pressure of some kind. However, the FBI made it clear to me that I should abandon any such attempt. Mama and *papa* were also, little by little, returning to their own lives and the only thing I could do was send letters to Cuba, something I haven't stopped doing all my life.

I was back in Miami and once again trapped. I couldn't do anything but go with the flow, conscious that the only thing I had achieved in trying to swim in the murky waters was to drown. Everyone implicated in Operation 40, and the numerous organisations with similar intentions against Fidel, loathed and despised me and didn't have any problem about letting me know. At the same time, they couldn't let me go because I was too involved and knew too much by now.

Ships, Arms and Flights
I intended to leave the Everglades and I looked for a job as a waitress but no more than a day went by before Frank Fiorini and some of his men turned up and I knew that I wouldn't be able to resist going back with them. Although the attempt on Fidel's life had failed, I was still useful.

The knowledge I had acquired with *papa* had made me one of the most skilled operators in the group for making the frequent sea voyages they undertook in that region to transport arms. Although at times I stayed at the hotel and cleaned or classified weapons, one of my most important activities for the group was reading the currents and tides. I could tell when storms were approaching and I was able to navigate. No talent was wasted and on several occasions I participated in the stealing of boats in places like Key West and Marathon Island where we unloaded weapons that then went on to Guatemala or Nicaragua where the tentacles of operations against Fidel extended, as they did in New Orleans in the United States.

The sea crossings were my main activity and, although they were stolen boats loaded with arms, for me they represented the opportunity for brief moments of happiness. Less liberating was one of the other tasks I carried out in those days: transporting arms by road that we had occasionally stolen from military armouries, which I did a couple of times with Fiorini. While I understood that we were stealing boats moored at mansions in Miami, I couldn't understand why, if the government was supporting what we were doing in Florida, we had to steal from the army. But I had spent enough time with the group to know that it was better not to ask questions, although I always had the suspicion that some of the cases of weapons were exchanged for drugs.

During those robberies my job was simple: on arriving at the armoury, a military installation that housed an excessive quantity of weapons, I had to stay with the car while Frank and his men carried out the theft, or I had to sweet-talk the police if they stopped us when we were carrying a load. Once, I had to distract the guards who were on watch. I got out of the car and pretended

146

the car had broken down. It was a way of starting a conversation that allowed me to flirt a bit. Then Frank and the others would break into the armoury while the guards were busy with me and they got what they had come for.

There was also an occasion when I went with Frank in one of the light aircraft that left Florida to drop leaflets over Cuba, sheets of paper full of propaganda urging Cubans to rise up against Fidel. Alex Rorke had also gone out with Frank on another flight when they dropped 250,000 sheets of anti-Castro literature over the island and he was questioned by the FBI about it. The interrogation surprised him because the CIA office in Miami was aware of Fiorini's activities which he claimed were direct orders from the Agency in Washington. In fact, Alex assured them that if he and Frank were arrested at any time by a unit operating under the law who didn't know anything about their activities, all they needed to do was give the agents a telephone number for their contact in the CIA office in Miami who would explain their role. Just in case, Alex also had an ace up his sleeve — his best press contacts which he had developed through his work as a freelance journalist and photographer. He had also agreed to a plan with Frank to embarrass Agency officials who tried to distance themselves from them if they were arrested. However, I just let them take me along with them and, when I flew with Fiorini, the one thing I did was enjoy writing my own messages on a handful of pamphlets. I scribbled phrases like 'I love you, Fidel' or 'Viva Cuba, LIBRE!' and I signed them 'La Alemanita'. It was childish, I know, but it makes me smile, even today.

A Woman in a Man's World

Although I could have moments of immaturity, I was also stronger and more confident, although it was really only a question of survival. I was the only woman in a world dominated by men and, although I was never the victim of any sexual aggression when I was in Florida, I decided to draw a line that would function as a brake to any potential overdose of testosterone. On one occasion, when we were in the Everglades, where the humidity and mosquitoes were stultifying and the discomfort almost unbearable, some of the men started to make jokes about me. I felt trapped; all I wanted to do was put on clean clothes and put my hair in curlers and I was in no mood for jokes or uncalled-for comments so I climbed up on top of a lorry and fired some shots into the air.

'If anyone is thinking about coming into my tent, I won't be pointing in the air the next time I pull the trigger,' I announced from my improvised platform.

The message had the desired effect and was enough of a show for them to understand that I wasn't just a woman there but one of them. No one ever dared to come into my tent in the camp in the Everglades.

Frank always treated me as one of the men during my time with the group, without making any kind of distinction between me and the rest of the guys. However, not everyone seemed to understand why I was still there after the episode with the two pills that were thrown in the bidet. Perhaps someone wanted to remind me that I was vulnerable. That would explain what happened during one the training camps when a bullet that someone fired at my shoulder grazed the nape of my neck. The bullet didn't penetrate my neck but the wound bled a lot and because the profuse bleeding was more than expected during the night, Frank decided to send me to Miami to Orlando Bosch's house. He was one of the most rabid anti-Castro activists of the period and some years later he was accused, with Luis Posada Carilles, of planning the attack on a Cuban plane in 1976, flying between Barbados and Jamaica, in which seventy-three people died.

In those days, Bosch was, for me, just another Cuban exile who was part of Fiorini's group. I had seen them together several times and that day he was my salvation. Although he was a paediatrician, his medical knowledge and the equipment he kept at home was enough to ensure that I didn't have to go to hospital where, by law, the authorities had to be informed if anyone came in with a gunshot wound. I was alive but I didn't know if the shot had been fired by accident, whether the inaccuracy of the person firing the gun had saved me, or if someone was intentionally giving me a warning. None of the three options gave me any peace of mind.

Another person I saw with Fiorini from time to time was someone I knew as 'Eduardo', a white man who I remember as a dark shadow, and he became a familiar face. The first time I saw him was in 1960 in the Brickle Garden apartments in Miami. A few of us were in a car and Frank said that he had to go and collect something. When he got out of the car he met this man who gave him an envelope. They repeated the meetings and the handing over of envelopes dozens of times, perhaps on more than thirty occasions, and although we didn't know who he was, we were all aware that when Frank and 'Eduardo' saw each other, money changed hands which allowed us to keep going. Years later, when the Watergate scandal broke and Fiorini/Sturgis was arrested, I discovered the real name and the importance of the mysterious 'Eduardo'. It was E. Howard Hunt, security adviser in Nixon's White House whose telephone number was found in the address book of those arrested at the Democratic Party campaign offices. Hunt had been a CIA agent since 1949 and had helped plan the secret operation which removed President Jacobo Arbenz from power in Guatemala, leading to forty years of military dictatorship in this Central American country. When I saw him in Florida, he was financing the preparations for the invasion of the Bay of Pigs.

From Anticipation to Failure: The Bay of Pigs

Sometimes military advisers also came to the hotel in Miami and to the Everglades. They didn't just train the youngsters there but also gave talks and lectures to encour-

151

age them, boost their morale and teach them the art of patience. However, this last part of the lesson didn't seem to get through to them. At the beginning of 1961, when there was no training in the Everglades, they spent the majority of the time waiting and listening to the same anxious question repeated over and over again: 'When will the day come?'

The fact that D Day never arrived was, in good part, down to people involved in the group itself because all you could hear was a lot of conversations expressing hatred for Fidel, against communism and about the invasion plans. Perhaps if they hadn't taken so much cocaine while they were in this 'army', the level of nervousness and indifference would have been reduced and the leaks less detrimental to their goals. The plans were discussed by everyone. Even the media published stories openly describing what was going on in Florida and, of course, Cuba didn't lack information about this impending threat. In fact, as everyone talked so much about it they had to delay the launch of the operation several times and created a number of false alarms.

In any case, as far as I was concerned everything they were planning was stupid and I had a whole host of doubts, partly because I had lived in Cuba where I had seen the majority of the population supported Fidel and it didn't seem likely to me that the 'rebels' were going to get support from the inside, which was absolutely vital if they were to accomplish the plan of ousting the regime once they landed on the island and started the invasion. I knew one of the designated points for disembarkation, the Zapata Swamp, very well as I had visited it with Fidel. I knew that the plan wouldn't work and that many of them would drown. I told them they were mad if they thought they could land their launches there.

Finally, on 17 April 1961, they launched the alleged invasion of Cuba in the Bay of Pigs. As much as the Secretary of State, Dean Rusk, denied that the US government was involved in the situation, the whole world knew that those 1,500 men who tried to face up to 30,000 of Fidel's soldiers were trained by the CIA and it was later officially confirmed that the Agency had formulated the plan in 1960 during the Eisenhower administration which was then approved by John F. Kennedy after he was told about it when he won the elections in November that year, destroying Nixon. In reality, Kennedy had known about the plot before, when he was just candidate in the presidential election, and he used it as a political weapon. Knowing that the plans had to be kept secret and that Nixon couldn't speak publically about them, the Democratic candidate torpedoed his rival in statements and debates, saying that he was doing nothing to stop Castro, and Nixon, his hands tied, couldn't deny it as such, nor avoid looking weak in his handling of Havana.

President Kennedy gave the invasion plans the green light in February 1961 which included two air attacks on Cuban bases before the arrival of the 'exiles' army, Brigade 2506, which would sail from Guatemala. The first of the air attacks took place on 15 April and not only did it fail but it left Fidel's air force almost entirely intact and also allowed images of obsolete American B-26 bombers to be seen which, with the help of the CIA, had been repainted to try to pass for Cuban planes. The Ambassador for the United States at the United Nations, Adlai Stevenson II, tried to defend the assertion that it was an internal revolution and to prove the point he showed a photograph of the repainted planes without realising that the photographs confirmed absolutely that they had tried, unsuccessfully, to disguise the aircraft. Under growing pressure against the undeniable involvement of Washington, Kennedy suspended the second wave of bombings that was due to take place.

On the 17th, close to 1,300 members of Brigade 2506 arrived at the Bay of Pigs and immediately found themselves under intense Cuban fire which left them isolated, sunk support ships and brought down planes that were meant to provide air support. Fidel intensified the siege, causing the failure of an emergency air mission authorised by Kennedy and, on the 19th, the attempt to change the regime on the island crumbled. Around 100 exiles were killed and close to 1,200 captured. In three days, Fidel successfully stopped a so-called invasion. Meanwhile, for Kennedy the problems were just beginning. It didn't matter that the 'abandonment' that Cuban exiles and members of Brigade 2506 reported would have been, for the most part, the responsibility of the CIA. The hatred of the anti-Castro movements and other participants involved in destabilizing Fidel immediately changed course and was directed towards the occupant of the White House.

The Venezuelan General
The only thing that the spectacular failure of the Bay of Pigs succeeded in doing was

to strengthen Fidel and move him even closer to the Soviet Union. However, or perhaps because of this, anti-Castro activities didn't stop in the United States, although it had increased hatred of Kennedy. Fiorini and his 'assassination group' hadn't participated personally in the invasion and had stayed in the rearguard. Frank started to entrust less dangerous missions to me such as stealing arms or moving armaments, as well as those where I collected money or information from 'donors' to the cause. With this in mind, in May 1961 he sent me to 4609 Pine Tree Drive, a mansion in Miami beach. The only thing he had said to me was that the donor in this case was a 'retired General' and that he would give me his contribution during a party. I had to go to the house, collect the bag with the money and leave. Frank would be waiting outside in the same car that had taken me there.

I rang the bell and two of the 'General's' bodyguards drove me to the house passing a garage containing eleven cars, including an extravagant white Mercedes with red interior. Each step was moving me into a world of obvious luxury, with the entire garden full of beautiful palm trees. As I heard the music from the party, I thought, 'how fortunate this General is. It looks like he lives well.'

When we reached a part of the property that wasn't the main entrance, they left me waiting in a room. I felt stupid sitting there on my own near people who were enjoying themselves at the party which sounded glorious, even more so to someone who had spent the last few months in swamps and motels, covered in mud, surrounded by weapons and being eaten to death by mosquitoes. Those were my thoughts when 'the retired General' arrived and greeted me with a simple hello. He was short, like the actor Danny DeVito. He looked adorable to me and although he was fat and was losing his hair, he had a sweet smile which lit up his face. I stood up to greet him and, getting straight to the point, told him that I was there to collect a bag. I was sure that he would know what I was referring to. He didn't show any signs of going to get it but invited me to sit down and asked:

'Are you German?'

It seemed that he knew more about me than I knew about him and this worried me a bit. It didn't change when all he said in those first few moments was that his name was Marcos. Then he got up and left. He didn't come back with the money but with a tray with two glasses and a bottle of Rhine wine instead. Although I refused his invitation to have a drink, he poured a glass and started to ask me questions and to flirt with me. I was slightly worried, thinking that Frank was outside waiting for me and I reminded my host that I was there only to collect what I had been sent to get. I also told him that they were waiting for me outside the gates to the house. He answered assertively and sharply:

'Let them wait.'

I had the impression that whatever was happening was out of my control in this instance so I decided to accept a glass of wine. I didn't expect Marcos to be so bold so quickly, touching me and sliding across the red sofa next to me. I tried to move away and reminded him again that there were people waiting for me outside and that he had something to give me. He threw in the towel and stopped making advances towards me but he made it clear that this would not be our last meeting.

When he said, 'I have to see you again', part question part demand, something sounded familiar, an echo of what Fidel had said to me before leaving the *Berlin* after our first meeting. Marcos insisted that I go out with him, go out to dinner and see him again. He told me that he had heard a lot about me and I ended up giving in and saying, 'perhaps, one day' and he seemed satisfied with that. He let me go, gave me the bag and I left. When I left the house I was very happy to see Frank's car still sitting here and I breathed a sigh of relief. I didn't really want to walk alone through the streets of Miami with more than $400,000 on me. Once I was back in the car, I asked Frank who the hell I had just met and he laughed.

'He keeps us going. That's the General of Venezuela. You've just met another dictator.'

I didn't find that particularly amusing but I started to ask who this 'General' was. I knew nothing about Venezuela or its politics despite having docked there on some of my trips with *papa*. He seemed a pretty brazen individual and I was pleased that I had resisted his advances. However, I had to admit that, despite his audacity, I thought he had been nice. He had a firm handshake and I had liked his smile. I felt he was sincere and that he really did want to see me again.

Flying Solo

I decided to try to break away from the life I was leading, to distance myself from covert operations, military training camps, robbery, assassinations and fruitless attempts to invade other countries and try to fly solo. It therefore seemed appropriate to move towards this objective by signing on with the Pan Am training school, the airline which had been established to fly passengers and mail between Key West and Cuba, and at the beginning of the 1960s it was the principal airline in the United States. It offered a six-week course for training as an air hostess. I spoke some Spanish as well as German and English and I began the course with great enthusiasm, knowing that once I had completed it there would be a job that I really liked waiting for me.

One day when I was coming out of class I noticed a small figure on the other side of the road whom I recognized immediately. He meant what he said at our first meeting about wanting to see me again. After greeting each other, he invited me to go out with him. I agreed and we went to a fish restaurant; we had a good conversation while we ate, nothing about politics or Cuba or Venezuela, nothing about money or Frank. More than anything, I listened.

Marcos started to turn up at the school more frequently to pick me up and take me for walks. In those first few dates he was always polite but he also wanted to touch me and I refused to let him — or at least I did at the start until I got used to him. Mama had always said to me that I shouldn't go out alone with men and that I shouldn't be deceived by presents because the only thing they wanted in return for them was my body. But I ignored all Alice's advice when I was with Marcos. On one of our dates he took me to a Polynesian restaurant where he gave me an 18-carat gold bracelet. Dangling from it was a coin showing his face and an inscription on both sides which read 'Presidents of Venezuela'. I couldn't stop myself laughing: this fat little man who usually wore Bermuda shorts and tennis shoes to go out with me was on a gold coin.

In the days that followed the dates and the presents continued: pearls from Isla Margarita, white gold and yellow gold jewellery of various carats . . . With each present he gave me he took the opportunity to tell me something about his country and its beauty and I gradually began to put together a picture of Venezuela and of him. He invariably boasted about his beautiful country and how much he had done for it, listing the motorways, public buildings and homes for the poor that he had built. He said nothing about his being a dictator notorious for his brutality and corruption.

161

A member of the government between 1948 and 1952, he promoted himself to General and proclaimed himself President in 1952. Marcos Pérez Jiménez ruled Venezuela with a rod of iron politically, but with a lighter touch when it came to public funds, until a coup *d'état* forced him to flee in 1958. He was held responsible for brutally eliminating political enemies such as Leonardo Ruiz Pineda and Antonio Pinto Salinas, forcing hundreds of others into exile or imprisoning and torturing them in infamous places such as the prison colony in Guasina. Nor did Marcos mention Pedro Estrada, the man always by his side in Miami, who had been the head of the feared National Security. I once asked him how many people he had killed and he gave me brief and evasive answers, saying things like:

'If you have a rotten apple, you have to get rid of it because if you don't the whole basket will rot and you have to get rid of all them.'

He didn't talk about how much money he had taken out of the country either, although it has been calculated that he stole hundreds of millions. Rómulo Betancourt, who succeeded him as President, presented formal charges: in addition to four political assassinations, there were charges for the theft of $13.5 million. Although it was believed that Pérez Jiménez had taken much more out of the country, that was the amount they found together with incriminating documents in a suitcase he left behind when he left hurriedly for the Dominican Republic on 23 January 1958.

After spending three months on the island, which was then under the thumb of his friend and fellow dictator Rafael Leónidas Trujillo, he went into exile in Miami. Shortly after his arrival in 1959, Caracas formally requested his extradition. Marcos posted bail of $100,000 for his release and was living the life of luxury in Florida of which I had just begun to be aware. However, behind the opulence there were also reminders of a darker reality and, since the petition for extradition had been formalised, he had to present himself on the first Monday of every month at the offices of the US Immigration and Naturalization Service.

That was the man who had set his heart on me and who sometimes came to find me at the guerrilla hotel where, to my regret, I was still living. I was still unable to live independently of Frank's group until I didn't get the job as an air hostess. Marcos said he would help me get out of there and leave the group and he gave me the money in advance for a year's rent on the apartment where I was living with Margarita Flaquer, a friend I had met in the classes and who I had moved in with. Margarita lived with a Cuban and her place was a very pretty apartment just over a bridge. That was where I first slept with Marcos one day when my friend had gone out with her boyfriend and I drank too much sparkling wine.

Sex with him wasn't wonderful or even good. I certainly couldn't compare it to sex with Fidel. Marcos wasn't a good lover. He was selfish and, for him, sex was just a function, not something to give yourself up to and lose yourself in. What he really liked was being romantic.

The Wrong Relationship

After that first sexual encounter I tormented myself with questions about why I had done it, telling myself that I didn't really love him. But he was fun and sweet and had a brilliant, contagious smile. I learned from him something I hadn't known before: how to grow alongside someone, to love and be loved. Ours was a good relationship, solid and affectionate, although it was also wrong. Marcos was married to a woman called Flor

Chalbaud, with whom he had four daughters.

He was also jealous. Several weeks into our relationship and a few days before I was to get my qualification from Pan Am, he saw me dressed in my blue uniform and all his insecurities came out. He made it clear that he didn't want me to go ahead with it, complaining that I would be spending all day being stared at by men. I had already been on a training flight to Rio de Janeiro and I loved the idea of becoming an air hostess but there was nothing I could do to prevent my dreams evaporating once again. And they didn't do so just because of Marcos's jealousy.

One day, on one of my flights with Pan Am, I felt ill, sick, the same feeling I had experienced in Cuba. The signs were obvious, although I was surprised, found it hard to believe and told myself that it couldn't be what I thought it was. I didn't use any protection or take precautions when I had sex with my new lover because my mother had never taught me anything about sex education, contraceptives or family planning and I had also believed what they had told me so many times in New York. I wasn't able to have children because of the botched operation in Cuba which had destroyed my body and had left me sterile. I now had conclusive evidence that everything they had told me was a pack of lies: Marcos had made me pregnant.

When I gave him the news, he was happy and started to make arrangements, finding me a gynaecologist in Miami, for example, who attended me through the pregnancy; this was Harry P. Wolck, whose practice was in Brickle Avenue. It was clear that I couldn't continue with Pan Am and it didn't only feel sad giving up this course but it also frightened me because I didn't know if I would be able to survive. Marcos calmed me down, assuring me that he would look after everything. 'Everything will be all right' was a phrase that he often repeated at that time.

In spite of the happiness we both felt, the pregnancy was the spark that ignited the rivalry Marcos felt towards Fidel, whom he hated profoundly. I had never told him much about my previous relationship but Marcos knew about it in detail and sometimes, when he was with me and had had too much to drink, he made abusive telephone calls to Fidel in Havana in which he began by boasting that he now had Fidel's girlfriend and he had made her pregnant. A commonplace when he was drunk, such calls became so frequent that one day secret agents approached me and asked me to urge Marcos to stop making calls to Cuba.

They also approached me at home a couple of times, at the request of Fiorini. They wanted to see how I was but, above all, they had to ask lots of questions about Marcos. I tried to get rid of them, explaining that I had left the group but I couldn't stop it and I became frightened when they started to threaten me during one visit. Once, for example, a man appeared who I have never seen before but whose face I remember perfectly because he had a problem with one of his eyes. This guy, who frightened me, urged me to leave the house and my lover and I have always believed that he wanted to kidnap Marcos to get some money.

Aside from the visits, which were a reminder of a past that was impossible to leave behind, my life in those months was quiet and I devoted my days to pastimes such as doing puzzles or listening to music. I went shopping with Margarita and waited around for Marcos, who visited me a couple of times a week, telling them at home that he was playing tennis. Marcos was an unfaithful husband and very discreet, a skill developed through experience. He hid his activities perfectly, so much so that Flor Chalbaud didn't know that he was conducting a loving, sexual relationship with me nor that I was expecting a baby with her husband.

A Mother's Comfort

No one in my family knew I was pregnant again and I wanted to tell my mother. However, when I rang home I didn't speak to her but to Joe instead. I brought him up to date with my situation and, when he learned who the father was, he started screaming at me. JoJo described Marcos as a murderer, one of the cruellest dictators who had ever existed and a monster, accusations that I had heard and read before but which seemed at odds with the man I knew intimately. Even more so, he made me feel frightened and it revived the ghost of memories of what had happened in Cuba. I felt genuine terror thinking about it and I was afraid that perhaps someone would want to take my baby from me again. I was so terrified that I froze and I hardly left the house. When I got to the eighth month of my pregnancy, I only went out of the house accompanied by Marcos's bodyguards to go to the doctor's.

The anxiety was too much for me and I

didn't want to be alone at the end of my pregnancy. I needed to speak to mama who was then working as a secretary at Cadwalader, Wickersham & Taft, an international law firm based on Wall Street. When we finally spoke, the conversation was tense and bitter and I remember the details of that call as if it had happened today. It was a very one-sided conversation full of recriminations on her part for my not having followed her advice to keep my distance from men and explosive fury when she found out that the father of the baby I was expecting was Pérez Jiménez. In mama's eyes, Marcos was the same as Fidel and it didn't matter that I reassured her that this time things were different and this man loved me and wasn't going to leave me and nothing was going to happen to me or my baby and that he would look after us. It was almost worse telling her that and I'll never forget her furious shouting, during which she screamed:

'You're a kept woman!'

Instead of making my mother happy, I saw myself condemned again and I couldn't stop crying, at which point Marcos took the phone to try to reason with her.

'Alice, don't worry. I'll look after Marita. I'll look after her and the baby and I'll do everything right. Stop shouting, Alice. Stop

169

shouting.'

In that dramatic telephone conversation, mama insisted that I came north to stay with her and threatened to send someone to come and get me if I didn't do it. Marcos and I had a long, calm chat and we agreed that I would live with her in New Jersey and have our baby there. Almost nine months pregnant, I travelled with his bodyguards and when I arrived at 206 Wilson Avenue in Fort Lee, I met up with mama again and all the recriminations, screaming and tension disappeared. We hugged each other, we cried and we were happy.

Mama rented a ground-floor flat where she worked so that she could be with me all the time and go to the doctor with me. Marcos called every day and his bodyguards were put in charge of a tennis club that he owned in the state. They frequently came round with food and presents. In those calls Marcos told me that I had to go and see Roy Cohn who was a big Mafia lawyer, a gangster who was going to set up a fund of $75,000 for me and another for the same amount for the baby who would also have a separate account for her education, medical expenses and other necessities. Marcos was keeping his promise and reassuring us that he would look after us.

With Alice and Heinrich Lorenz, my parents, a little after my birth in 1939.

After the war, my mother worked as a personal assistant to an American soldier, Major Davis. It was her first contact with espionage work that would soon form part of her life.

Smiling (bottom right) next to my mother, my sister Valerie and my brothers Philip and Joachim in a family portrait.

The rape that I was a victim of when I was little more than seven years of age turned me into an introverted child.

My sister Valerie and I in front of a North American army store in Bremerhaven, Germany, in 1945.

Many of my formative years were spent on board the ships my father captained.

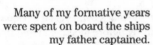

The *Berlin*, the first passenger ship that started to run the regular route between Europe and the United States after the war. Pictured arriving in Havana in 1959.

On the black sand beach in Cuba in 1959, shortly before meeting Fidel.

In the picture, from bottom to top, my mother, my father, a passenger and me on one of the ships that *papa* worked on.

Heinrich Lorenz, *papa*, photographed on board the *Berlin* with the Mayor of New York, Robert Wagner.

When the 'barbudos', led by Fidel, wanted to board the ship, I told them that they could come on board but I insisted they leave their weapons.

After a visit round the different areas of the *Berlin*, Fidel, *papa* and the others went to the first class restaurant. The other passengers were curious and approached Fidel to ask for his autograph.

Fidel's 'barbudos' mixed with first class passengers next to my father's table in the restaurant.

In 1959, Fidel went to the United States. Fidel is next to Vice President Richard Nixon in this photograph. (© Topham Picturepoint – Getty Images)

One of my favourite photos of Fidel. They took him to the Bronx Zoo. For me it represents the perfect metaphor for him – a majestic and fierce animal that understands the tragedy of a loss of liberty. (© Korda/Jazz Editions/ Contacto)

I was with Fidel for the whole of that trip. I wore
the uniform of the 26th of July Movement to fit
in with the others. I was a woman who was very
much in love and jealous.

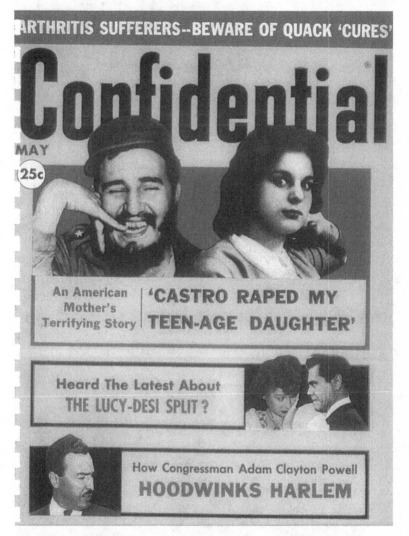

With the aim of defaming Fidel, Alex Rorke came up with the idea for an article for *Confidential* in which my mother claimed that Fidel had abused me.

With Frank Sturgis, the man who introduced me to the world of espionage. In 1972, he was arrested in relation to the Watergate scandal.

OUR TRIPLE-AGENT IN HAVANA

Sturgis, American spy and counter-spy, during his time as a guerrilla soldier in Cuba. After Watergate, he felt betrayed by the same authority that he had spent decades working for.

Sturgis standing with Frank Nelson (with glasses), who was responsible for the spy's finances and was a great enthusiast of the 'army' that he organised to assassinate Fidel.

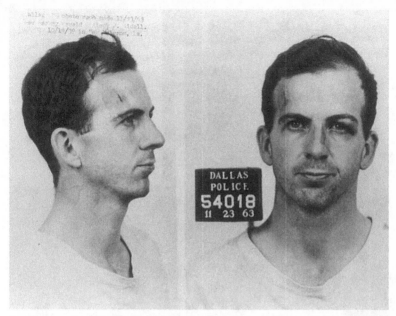

Lee Harvey Oswald, the presumed assassin of John F. Kennedy, photographed after his arrest. (© Corbis-Cordon Press)

Moments before Jack Ruby would shoot Lee Harvey Oswald at point blank range in the stomach, which would eliminate one of the key witnesses in the investigation of the assassination. (© Corbis-Cordon Press)

Marcos Pérez Jiménez, former President of Venezuela, was the father of my daughter, Monica Mercedes Pérez Jiménez. (© Courtesy of Fundación Andrés Mata)

'Everything is going to be alright', Marcos said to me when he found out I was pregnant.

With my daughter, Monica. Her father couldn't spend much time with her before they imprisoned him and extradited him to Venezuela.

The day they sent Marcos to Caracas, I wanted to say goodbye but they handcuffed me to the steering wheel of the car so that I couldn't hug him. (© Topfoto – Getty Images)

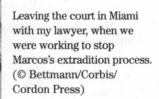

Leaving the court in Miami with my lawyer, when we were working to stop Marcos's extradition process. (© Bettmann/Corbis/ Cordon Press)

I carried on being the spy that, like it or not, I had always been. In the photo, taken in 1980, I am registering to work with the Cuban refugees that arrived in the United States that same year.

Family snaps
show Monica,
Mark, Louis
Yurasits and me.

Girl Buys Gun to Shield Mother, an Ex-CIA Spy

By PAUL MESKIL

A frightened 15-year-old girl bought a loaded pistol Monday in a desperate attempt to protect her mother, ex-spy Marita Lorenz, from Watergate burglar Frank Sturgis.

Detectives picked up the girl, with the automatic in her pocket, as she waited near her mother's Yorkville home for Sturgis to arrive. When Sturgis showed up a few hours later, he was arrested and charged with coercing Miss Lorenz to change her testimony before a congressional committee investigating the assassination of President Kennedy.

District Attorney Robert Morgenthau's office has been in contact with Manhattan U.S. Attorney Robert Fiske Jr.'s office to explore the possibility of pressing federal charges against Sturgis for allegedly harassing a federal witness, authorities said. However, the question of jurisdiction was not expected to be decided until today.

Miss Lorenz' daughter is Monica Mercedes Perez Jiminez. Both she and her mother gave The News permission to use her name. Monica's father, who has never contributed to her support, is former Venezuelan dictator Marcos

Perez Jiminez, a multimillionaire now living in Spain.

Miss Lorenz met Sturgis in 1959 while she was living in Havana with Cuban Premier Fidel Castro. Sturgis, then known as Frank Fiorini, was an officer in Castro's revolutionary army and a contract agent for the CIA.

He recruited Miss Lorenz to spy on Castro. Later, when both Miss Lorenz and Sturgis left Cuba, he allegedly sent her b[...]
first [...]
suite [...]
to ass[...]

Six[...]
News [...]
Harve[...]
trip f[...]
before [...]
ed in [...]
she re[...]
ing da[...]
Sh[...]

(C[...]

At 15 years old, Monica decided to confront Sturgis on her own. On 31 October 1977, she hid next to our apartment with a .22 calibre pistol with the aim of 'stopping him'.

Weapons had always been around me. I learned to use them very quickly.

Next to an officer and translator that I worked with at Fort Chaffee, Arkansas.

For a while, I worked in a centre for the treatment of compulsive gamblers that Valerie founded in Baltimore, Maryland.

Next to actors Gabrielle Anwar and Joe Mantegna in 1999 during the filming of *My Little Assassin,* based on my life with Fidel.

In the living room of my house with some of my pets – I love animals – with a photograph of my parents in the background.

Giving Birth in the Middle of a Storm

Although I was due to give birth in February, exactly three years to the day that I had first met Fidel, I can only be grateful that such a coincidence would not become an ironic reminder in my life and it wasn't until 8 March that I started to have contractions. With an ability for drama that seemed to hound me, there was a tremendous snow-storm in 1962 which was given the name 'the Ash Wednesday storm' and it went down in history as one of the ten worst storms of the twentieth century in the United States. It devastated six states along the Atlantic coast for three days, leaving dozens dead and millions of dollars lost. The hospital where I had planned to give birth was in Manhattan and mama and I lived in New Jersey. It was impossible to get hold of an ambulance so we had to go and find a police officer and, as with so many things in my life, the journey was an odyssey, like something out of a film, with mama hysterical, me in tears and the poor new police officer who had to take us on that journey begging me not to give birth in his car on one of his first jobs.

We reached the hospital and the following morning, on 9 March 1962, I gave birth to a large baby weighing four kilos. They had to use forceps and they didn't give me any kind of anaesthetic, which made the birth an agonising and heart-rending experience. However, when I heard my daughter's cries, all the suffering and agony was forgotten and I couldn't contain my emotion or happiness. In the previous pregnancy, the drugs stopped me feeling anything and this time the unbearable pain felt like a blessing. At last I had done it; I had brought a baby into the world, a small, living human being who was now lying in my arms.

The first call I had was from Marcos and I heard his voice on the other end of the phone, anxious and happy, asking how the boy was.

'It's a girl,' I told him, a little ashamed.

'Oh no! I don't want any more girls!' he exclaimed, disappointed.

'I'm sorry, I'm sorry, I made a girl,' I mumbled, apologising and unable to stop myself bursting into tears.

As she had done with her four children and her granddaughter, mama managed it so that the father had little say in the choice of a name. Marcos wanted our baby to be called Adela María after his mother but Alice came up with her own choice of name and my baby was called Monica. The only solace for Marcos was that my mother let him add Mercedes as her middle name.

Marcos took care of everything financially as well. We were in the New York Lion Hospital in a huge room with a view of the river, the same one that Jackie Kennedy occupied after giving birth to Caroline and, as I had no medical insurance, Marcos paid for everything and always in cash. It cost him between $10,000 and $20,000. He filled the entire room with flowers and sent presents, Lladró figurines, fruit . . . He also sent his bodyguards and insisted that one of them was always on guard at the window of the neonatal room. In the worlds in which we both moved, that fear of certain events or people might seem a little exaggerated but it was never completely unfounded. He was concerned that someone might try to swap babies.

After the birth and the stay in hospital, I went back to mama's house. She had an apartment on two floors and those were some of the happiest days of my life. I was amazed by my daughter. I couldn't stop looking at her for a second and loved her in a supremely unique way, learning and discovering something new and feeling astonished every minute of the day . . . She was fabulous, the most marvellous thing I had ever experienced. She allowed me to possess her through maternal feeling, love, amazement, incredulity and the magic of knowing that this creature had come out of my body, that she was mine. I only felt this ecstasy then and, again, years later when I had my son Mark. Obviously, I had to rely on the respective fathers in both cases to create them but there are certain life experiences that belong only to women.

I stayed with Alice for a couple of months, although I spoke to Marcos every day and missed him and all I wanted to do was go back to Miami to be with him. I know he missed me too and was impatient to get to know his daughter. He paid for a first-class air ticket so that we could go back to Miami where he would be waiting for us when we arrived and he rented a duplex for me near the canal. Everything in it was white: the leather, the carpets, the marble . . . He also employed a nurse not just to help me but to afford company for me because I was on my own much of the time. Marcos's wife, who had left Miami for Peru, had returned to the United States and he could only come and see us for a little while on some days.

If Flor Chalbaud had been the only challenge we faced in being together I think we would have overcome it but then Marcos's legal situation in the United States became much more complicated and the political forces creating these complications — publically and privately — were impossible to appease. Bobby Kennedy was US Attorney General at the time and was working with the Venezuelan president, Betancourt, who was putting pressure on him to get a successful extradition. It made little difference that, as a gesture of goodwill, Marcos had donated money to JFK's re-election campaign or that he had tried to establish some credibility as a good resident of the United States, also donating a million dollars to begin the construction of the Walt Disney World resort in Orlando. It was now being suggested that Marcos was in danger of fleeing the country, and his willingness to post bail of $300,000 had convinced no one that his intention was to remain in the United States.

David Walters, a former border agent with links to the CIA, was his lawyer and could find no way of halting the extradition, a situation that was causing Marcos to sink into depression so that Monica and I saw less and less of him. Finally, in December 1962, he was sent to Dade County prison, from which he phoned me every night after paying $300 in bribes to the guards for each call. And that was when I realised I was pregnant again.

The Most Hated Man

Walters, who was also managing the trust fund, moved me from the duplex in which Marcos had installed me when I came back to Miami to a suite in Bay Park Towers. I was a key player in the strategy he had come up with to try to stop Marcos's extradition. I didn't understand at the time that his plan would end up costing me a great deal of money and it was the start of a tortuous relationship with the lawyer that would reach the extremes of a pure and brutal hatred.

To avoid extraditing Marcos, he explained to me, we had to present a paternity suit so that, in theory, they couldn't make him leave the country while that was in progress. I was worried about something: in the trust fund agreement there was a confidentiality clause about paternity and if it went ahead it meant I could lose everything. But Walters tried to reassure me, telling me that nothing would happen and he found a lawyer, Montague Rosenberg, to begin the process. This man presented the papers for a case in which they decided, without my participation, that they would demand $5,000,000 from Marcos.

I was a pawn once again, a piece in a game played by others, a puppet whose strings moved at the whim of someone else. It was a discreet role in a work whose scope was beyond my understanding. In June 1963 two enormous men appeared at my door saying they came from the office of Bobby Kennedy and, without giving me an option, made me sit down and listen. They demanded that I withdraw the paternity suit. I tried to explain to them that I couldn't do so because it was the only thing that was keeping the man I loved in the United States and it was also my guarantee that he would still be alive; he was convinced that if he returned to Caracas, Betancourt would execute him. They listened to me but reiterated that, with or without me, Pérez Jiménez was going to be extradited. Then they put some papers in front of me and explained that if I signed them they would stop the judicial process. In exchange, they said, they would consider returning to me the funds that I would otherwise lose. I could see the strategy for that it was: a dirty trick, pure bribery. I refused to sign. That was the card I played. And I lost.

The judicial process continued and, in one of the sessions, Judge Wiseheart, who was presiding over the paternity suit, asked who the fund's anonymous donor was. Walters approached the judge and, speaking loudly enough so that several reporters in the courtroom could hear, gave the name of Marcos Pérez Jiménez. The confidentiality that was so essential for ensuring the security of the funds that Marcos had put aside for Monica and me blew up in our faces. We ended up without anything. Walters, that damned Walters, just said:

'Bad luck.'

To this day I hate him more than I have ever hated anyone.

My problems were going to be much more serious and painful that just being alone and penniless. The most horrible confirmation came when I was three months pregnant and went for a walk with Monica. A car, a red Chevy, came speeding up behind us. I just had time to push my daughter's pram out of the way to avoid it being hit but I couldn't save myself. The car drove off quickly after hitting me and left me bleeding. They took me to a medical centre where I had to have an operation. I knew the unthinkable had happened again. I had lost another baby.

General Carlos Pulido, a colleague of Marcos, came to see me in hospital and tried to console me, saying that at least I had Monica. He tried to calm me down, assuring me that I was going to be all right but it did nothing to arrest my fears when, after I asked him who could have committed such a cruel act on a fellow human being, he replied:

'You have to be very careful that no one finds Monica.'

In fact, Pulido took me to his house when they discharged me a couple of days after the attack and I lived there with my daughter for a while, terrified and afraid to go out. Although I didn't know for sure who was behind the attempted murder of my baby and the death of my unborn child, all my suspicions centred on Walters who had earlier tried to have me declared an unfit mother so that I would have to give up custody.

As Walters was Marcos's lawyer, it was difficult to avoid him. One day he made me come into the office to sign some papers which purportedly referred to the apartment that the General had been renting for me but when I turned the page I saw a document concerning me giving up custody of my daughter. I went mad when I discovered his vile attempt to deceive me. I wanted to kill him. I started to throw things at him and to swear at him. Then I shouted that I knew he was behind the attempt to kill me. I wasn't calling his bluff or lying: after my accident, a detective investigating the case revealed that a hire car had been used in the attack and that it had been contracted by someone called Frank Russo, from Chicago. On the day of my accident it wasn't Russo who was driving but an investigator from the office of Richard Gerstein, the State Attorney for Miami and also a former agent for the FBI and very close to Walters. The law firm for which Walters worked was called Walters, Moore and Costanzo and the last named was the connection to Chicago and Russo. Walters was taken aback and looked as if he couldn't believe that I could be capable of uncovering all of this. I didn't understand anything. Who wanted my daughter? What for? What harm could a little girl do to anyone? A puppet. That's how I felt. A teenager sitting in the waiting room of his office applauded furiously when I left. It was Margot, the eldest of Marcos's four legitimate daughters who, like me, hated Walters but at the same time depended on him.

I tried to tell Marcos what had happened with Walters but I couldn't talk to him openly about it because they listened in to all our conversations. On 12 August, at the end of an intense legal battle on several fronts over four years which twice went before the Supreme Court, the Secretary of State, Dean Rusk, approved the extradition of the father of my daughter, the first such extradition of a political figure at this level and an indication of the direction that the Kennedy administration was taking in contrast to that of Eisenhower, which had awarded Marcos the Legion of Merit, a military decoration, in 1952.

A short while later a meeting took place at the Miami airport between Bobby Kennedy, Walters and a representative for Betancourt. Although Judge Robert Anderson ordered against the extradition taking place if Marcos paid the bail of $300,000 referred to in the paternity suit, and although my lawyer tried to report this at the sheriff's office to stop them handing him over, on 17 August 1963 Marcos left the cell in which he had spent the last eight months and was escorted in handcuffs to Miami airport by a retinue of six cars full of marshals and state police where two crews, guards, officials, a doctor and a nurse had been waiting for the last five days at the insistence of the Department of State.

A telegram from Washington confirmed

that the United States could hand over custody of the detainee and, at 12.25, after walking down a corridor with thirty American and Venezuelan agents, Marcos Pérez Jiménez was put on the plane on which he would make his return flight to Caracas together with twelve agents. Only his daughter Margot, Monica and I were at the airport. Margot fell to her knees and cried. They handcuffed me to the steering wheel of a car when I tried to go and embrace him and say goodbye to him.

Fallen into Disgrace

In the days that followed, having moved back to the Pulidos' again, everything was frenetic. I couldn't stop crying, I didn't know what to do and I was constantly harassed by journalists. Then one of the judges who had taken part in one of Marcos's legal cases was killed in an explosion on his boat in Miami and I was really frightened. Someone was playing fast and loose with C-4 explosive and I was terrified. I felt absolutely alone and I couldn't turn to the people of Cuba who still didn't want anything to do with me so it occurred to me to turn to Alex Rorke.

'I'm in disgrace with Fiorini,' he confessed to me.

It was the last time I would hear from my darling Alex. On 24 September, the light aircraft in which he was flying from Fort Lauderdale in Florida disappeared over Cuba. In a press conference the week following his disappearance, Jacqueline, Rorke's wife, revealed that her husband's last flight had been financed by Luis Somoza, the former President of Nicaragua and a fervent anti-communist. Jacqueline was also sure that although Alex had told her that he was going to Managua to negotiate the opening of an import/export company with Somoza, he and Geoffrey Sullivan, the pilot with whom he had flown over Cuba a few days before to attack petrol refineries, had registered a flight plan in Florida with a destination of Panama. When they stopped to refuel in Cozumel (Mexico), they changed this flight plan and entered Tegucigalpa as the destination. The bodies of Alex, Sullivan and a third passenger, identified as Enrique Molina García, were never found.

CHAPTER 5
DALLAS, NOVEMBER 1963

Alone with my baby, trapped and penniless in Miami, I wanted to recoup the money that belonged to Monica and me so I began a lawsuit to try to reclaim the funds that Marcos had left for us. I turned to the courts on a couple of occasions but my case failed because they claimed I had infringed a confidentiality clause — although it wasn't me who brought the paternity case to stop the extradition process, and nor was it me who named Marcos to a judge so that all the reporters could hear it. The legal channel was no longer viable for me and all I could do was confront that damned traitor, Walters. I had to protect myself from whoever was trying to ride roughshod over my daughter and me but I also had to find ways of putting pressure on him so that he wouldn't threaten us and would return the money to me that I was sure he had kept. I didn't know anyone better than Fiorini to help me do that so I was forced to go back to him again.

I knew the Cubans still remembered me from the business with Fidel's pills and they didn't want anything to do with me, but I was sure that Frank would know how to manage them so that they wouldn't cause me any problems. He was my only hope and initially he didn't let me down. When I approached him, I explained my situation and asked him to help me. He let me start running a few errands and assignments for him and I stayed as close to him as possible in the hope that he could give some of his time to helping me.

And so it was that I became involved with the old team again. There was Pedro Díaz Lanz, Manuel Artime and a couple of others . . . Sometimes soldiers of fortune and 'donors' hung around, like Cardin and someone whose name I can't remember but I know he was the heir to an international business empire. I realised that after the Bay of Pigs fiasco in 1961 the discussion had changed radically and the hatred that had previously been directed at Fidel was now aimed at John F. Kennedy. Perhaps because they were mistaken in thinking that I hated the president's family because of the role that Bobby Kennedy had played in the deportation of Marcos, they didn't bother to hide their resentment or their accusations that Kennedy had been intimidated and had caused the failure of the invasion when he didn't provide the air support he had promised. They left no room for doubt: they wanted him dead.

One day I went to a meeting at the home of Orlando Bosch because I needed to talk to Frank about Walters. My mind was on my own thoughts and I didn't pay much attention to what was happening or the details of the conversation. I do remember that on that day in September or October Bosch's sons were also at the house and they were taken out of the room where the group had gathered. The curtains were drawn and they started getting out several maps which they unfolded on the table in the living room. They started drawing circles on the maps that had various points marked on them and I could see 'Dallas' written on them. I paid little attention to the conversation while I helped Bosch's wife serve coffee. I just thought it was about a new trip to transport or steal arms like so many others the group had carried out before, although I didn't really understand why they had to go to Texas and I didn't ask either. At the time, Walters was the only thing on my mind and although, on the one hand, I felt things had changed a lot for me personally and that being a mother had given me a new sense of responsibility that made me want to distance myself from any illegal activity, I desperately needed the money.

Lee Harvey Oswald

The meeting lasted about an hour. Aside from Frank and Bosch, there were a few others including a young man whom I had seen three or four times before in Florida in a safe house that Fiorini's group maintained in south-east Miami and also in the training camps in the Everglades. In fact, the young man and I had appeared in a group photograph — one of the photographs that Alex Rorke took of the members of Operation 40 in the Everglades before he vanished without a trace. As usual, I am the only woman.

I first met the young man, who was at the meeting at Bosch's house, in Miami where we were involved in tasks such as cleaning guns and preparing leaflets that were then dropped over Cuba from light aircraft. When he arrived, I asked Frank who he was and he said:

'He's going to be one of us. He'll play his part.'

Fiorini introduced him to me as Lee

Oswald. From the beginning, I called him Ozzie. Later, I found out his full name: Lee Harvey Oswald.

I didn't trust Ozzie from the start. The people in the Florida group knew each other well. We had a relationship based on trust and he felt like an outsider. The day we met, I joked with him that he didn't look strong enough to manage an M16 rifle. He looked weak, almost as if he was starving. He didn't like the comment at all because after that, when we met a few times at the training camps in the Everglades, he was cold and distant towards me. He came across as conceited and when he started to show off about the number of places he had been to around the world I started to reel off a long list of countries I had visited thanks to my trips with *papa*. He assured us that he spoke several languages, although it seemed to me that his Spanish left a lot to be desired. You could understand it but he spoke with a strong accent and he gave the impression that he had just gone round collecting phrases here and there.

After the meeting at Bosch's house with Ozzie, Fiorini and the others, I went back to the motel where I was living after I lost the house that Marcos had bought me. I stayed in touch with Frank until, in the middle of November, he told me that it was time to take the trip. I left my baby with Willie Mae Taylor, a black cleaner who had been helping me keep the apartment tidy and look after my daughter and, as I couldn't pay her, she said she would look after Monica at home with her own children. Later, the old team including Frank, Oswald, Pedro Díaz Lanz, Gerry Patrick Hemming, Bosch and I rendezvoused again at the Cuban doctor's house where we had first met to plan the trip to Dallas and we left in two old cars to make the journey west.

Frank was in my car, as was Hemming who complained constantly about how uncomfortable he was. He was tall and there wasn't enough room in the back of the car for his long legs because the floor of the car was packed with guns, as was the trunk. I thought we would be leaving them at various points along the way as we had with previous shipments we had made on other occasions. However, this time everything seemed more rigorous than usual. For example, we were instructed to wear normal clothes, no camouflage or anything that looked like military garb, and we were absolutely forbidden to speak Spanish. They stressed over and over again that we had to drive very carefully and calmly to avoid any

189

incidents or being stopped for traffic of-
fences and that we weren't to stop, even to
eat. In fact, we only stopped at drive-ins,
those restaurants where there's no need to
get out of the car and food is collected at a
window. There wasn't even time to stop and
sleep and my travelling companions took
turns to drive without stopping to rest.
Everyone looked like zombies on the journey, even when high on cocaine or speed.

At one point, I asked why we needed all
the guns we were carrying and someone
answered:

'Oh! They'll be useful.'

Someone else even joked:

'We're going to kill Kennedy.'

Of course, I didn't believe him.

The Man in White Socks

After two days on the road, we passed a sign
that read 'Welcome to Dallas' and I knew
we had arrived at our destination. We stayed
at a hotel on the outskirts of town where we
had two rooms, each with two double beds,
where we could also comply with the very
precise instructions to the letter. There was
a complete ban on speaking Spanish, it was
absolutely forbidden to make or receive
telephone calls or bring anyone back to the
room and you couldn't go out for any

reason at all, not even to eat. Food was delivered to make sandwiches. We moved in and brought in bags full of guns from the cars, leaving them in the rooms next to the beds.

During my time there, I saw someone turn up to speak to Frank. He was a middle-aged man, somewhere between stocky and tubby, wearing white socks and a dark jacket and trousers. His face was familiar and he looked like a gangster type, a bit of a thug compared to the people I was with. I realised that I had seen this man before in Cuba at the Hotel Riviera. I didn't know his name then in Havana nor when I saw him at the motel in Dallas but I found it out a few days later: it was Jack Ruby.

Frank went to meet him outside the room and when Ruby realised I was there I heard him remonstrate with Fiorini:

'What's that fucking broad doing here?'

I could hear them arguing loudly enough to follow their conversation, even though they were outside the room. When they finished talking and Frank came back in, he approached me and said that he didn't think it was a good idea for me to stay with them.

'I think I made a mistake. They don't want a woman involved.'

I replied that I had taken part in similar

191

jobs, to which he replied:

'Not like this.'

I didn't argue any more nor did I answer back. It didn't really make any difference to me if I left and, in fact, that's what I wanted to do. I didn't feel well. My period had started and I had strong menstrual cramps and no sanitary towels; I didn't have any privacy and I had spent the first night sleeping on the floor between the two beds because I didn't want to share a mattress with any of the men. I had realised from the beginning that they didn't want me there. But, more than anything, I wanted to go because I missed my daughter.

These feelings and the circumstances made it easy to make the decision to leave. Frank gave me some money to get a flight back to Miami and took me to the airport along with Gerry Patrick Hemming, who was angry and unhappy about the mission. I don't know where he flew to but I got a flight to Miami and as soon as I landed in Florida I went to collect Monica from Willie Mae who lived in Homestead where there was an old military base. I was horrified by what I discovered. My darling Willie Mae lived in extreme poverty with her eight children, in a shack with no drinkable water and with chickens everywhere. Little Monica slept on a bug-ridden mattress. Willie Mae made an effort to keep it all clean and washed and cooked outside the four decrepit walls but it was truly heart-breaking. I thanked her and gave her all the money I had on me. I picked up my daughter and, after a couple of nights in Miami, I decided to go back to my mother. I felt desperate in Miami, frightened and vulnerable and, in a city full of opposing factions, I was very conscious of the fact that I didn't like any of them.

On Friday 22 November, I took an Eastern Airlines flight which left Miami and should have arrived at Idlewild in New York. Halfway through the flight, the captain informed us that the plane had been redirected to Newark in New Jersey. All he said was that something had happened in Dallas, an emergency, but something shifted inside me and made me think the unthinkable. All I could think was:

'Oh, my God. I hope not.'

When I landed, mama was there to meet me; she came up to me and took her granddaughter in her arms saying something that confirmed my hunch, my worst fears:

'Someone shot Kennedy.'

Back at home in Fort Lee, we put the television on and, like millions of Americans, we were glued to the screen.

Two days later, after his arrest on the 22nd and claiming that he was a scapegoat, Lee Harvey Oswald was assassinated in the basement of the Municipal Prison in Dallas as he was being transferred to a maximum security cell in the prison where condemned men were held. The man who shot him while the cameras were transmitting the transfer live to the whole country was the foul-mouthed man I had seen in the Hotel Riviera in Cuba and who had become so agitated when he saw me in the motel in Dallas: Jacob Leonard Rubenstein, also known as Jack Ruby.

I told mama that I had been in Dallas. She told Frank Lundquist and Frank O'Brien who came to the house several times, questioned me and showed me photographs from which I identified everyone I knew. I didn't think about it until fifteen years later, in 1978, when I was called to testify before the House Select Committee on Assassinations in the House of Representatives which investigated the murders of John F. Kennedy and Martin Luther King and where I related what I have written here. I didn't think about it much in the years that followed because that trip was only two days out of my life. Although everyone says it's very important, that I was close to those who did it and that I have information about the assassination, I don't know anything else other than what I've just said here. Was I close to them? Yes, but I was always on the edge of things. I know that Fiorini, Bosch and the others said they wanted JFK dead. I'm sure they weren't the only ones but they are the only ones I heard say that.

CHAPTER 6
SAFE IN THE RAINFOREST

In a country where you can kill a president and never know who is really responsible for the assassination, a life isn't worth much and the life of someone like me, who has been involved with forces that move in the shadows and for whom there are no borders, either legal or illegal, is worth even less.

On the way back from the trip to Dallas, and after my umpteenth passage through Miami, I had decided to continue living with mama in Fort Lee and I found a job at Prentice Hall, a publisher of education books. It was my fourth 'ordinary' job after my time with Pan Am, the brief attempt to be a waitress after returning to Cuba after the episode with the pills and a post that I had in the 1950s paying the stevedores at the shipping company that *papa* worked for, Norddeutscher Lloyd. But very soon it became clear to me that it wasn't going to be so easy to survive by working in an office. One day at work I felt a touch on the shoulder and when I turned round I saw a couple of detectives next to me and two others waiting. They asked me to accompany them and my first thoughts were that something had happened to Monica. I was terrified and the first thing I wanted to do was to ask them about her.

'Where is my daughter? Is she all right?'

They reassured me immediately but they didn't want to alarm the other employees so they asked me if we could go outside. Once we were outside the publishing offices, they told me that they had received a telegram from the office of a sheriff in Florida advising that he had come across a car containing five individuals on their way to New Jersey who intended to do something to my daughter and me. Monica and I were targets for someone once again but it was impossible to work out who. I immediately thought that it had to be Walters again, the only person I knew for certain had tried to kill us, but it could also have been the Cubans in exile, or even Frank or someone who was still feeling uneasy about me and who had been in the Dallas convoy.

Although the car identified by the sheriff had been stopped somewhere in Virginia, I knew, again, that I wouldn't have any peace and that my plans for a serene, quiet and normal life would evaporate without me being able to do anything about a threat that I couldn't even identify. That uncertainty and the reality of the danger made me reluctantly accept the protection I was offered by the authorities who put mama, Monica and me in a safe house in New Jersey while they carried out their investigations. The supposed protection was, for me, more like a prison and, although they gave my mother permission to go out to work, I had to remain in the house and I couldn't go any further than the end of the garden. It went on for days and days, weeks, my first experience of a very claustrophobic and asphyxiating life in which you had to swap freedom for security, where staying alive was the price you paid for stultifying boredom and where it wasn't for you to say enough is enough.

Finally, after several weeks, they allowed me to leave custody and get my life back although not my peace. Despite bringing the investigation to an end, they never told me who the men in the car were or who had sent them. I was back at square one again.

I moved in for a while with my brother Philip, who had a brownstone near Central

Park. He took me to his concerts and was responsible for protecting me, together with JoJo and mama. My family were my salvation again but, despite their help, I felt lost. I depended on them and, to my shame, I had no money and I couldn't go back to Miami. I didn't know what to do with my life. I wanted to be invisible. However, I had a daughter now and I had to keep moving forward, not just for me but for her as well. I began to convince myself that the only way to go was to try to see Marcos again, explain to him everything that had happened with Walters and find a solution. To do it, I would have to go to Caracas where he was imprisoned and going to Venezuela became my goal: I would go there with Monica, no matter what.

I told Frank Fiorini about my plans and when he heard them he thought I was mad, but I made it clear that it was my only option and that at this point I had absolutely nothing to lose either. Although I was well aware that Walters wasn't my ally but my enemy, I also called him to try to get him to give me money to finance my trip. As I expected, he refused. It was mama, once again, who helped me. She was against me going and said repeatedly that it was a bad idea. However, she eventually gave me the money so that I could take the flight.

'Be Very Careful in Caracas'

When I embarked with Monica, I never had the feeling that we were alone. It always seemed to me that someone was watching us. It proved to be more than paranoia or unfounded fears when, just before taking his seat behind me in the cabin, a man came up very close to me and whispered:

'Be very careful in Caracas.'

The warning took me by surprise. Who should I be careful of in a city and a country where I didn't know anyone? What did I have to protect myself from? I didn't know who the man was and I never did find out, but he made sure that worry was my companion on that flight.

Once we had landed and as soon as I got off the plane I was surrounded by four men from SIFA, the Venezuelan military intelligence. Two were in uniform and two in plainclothes. Asking no questions, they insisted I accompany them. At first I thought it was a routine check so I made it clear that I had nothing to declare. I explained, with absolute honesty, that I had travelled to Venezuela to see Pérez Jiménez but they didn't seem interested in anything

200

I had to say to them and just wanted to carry out their orders. They only responded with one-word answers and only told me where we were going after I insisted several times,

'Don't you want to see Marcos? That's where we're going.'

They put me in a car with my baby and took us directly from the airport to the Modelo prison, a military institution in the middle of the city at the foot of the mountains at El Ávila Park. Two men in suits, both very polite and friendly, met us there and I went into the prison with them. It was a building with a beautiful garden in the middle. They knew who we were and, somehow, had known when my daughter and I would be arriving in Caracas. I assumed that they knew why I had made the trip and, as we all went upstairs to the second floor to an area where there were cells, I thought they were taking me to see Marcos.

I was wrong. They asked me if I would wait and someone appeared who introduced himself as Captain Durán. After that, the men in suits opened the door of one of the cells and ushered me inside with Monica. I didn't understand what was happening or why they wanted to lock me up but I was so tired from the journey that I didn't even ask any questions and I just walked into the cell. When Captain Durán took Monica and they closed the door of the cell, leaving me on my own, I was frightened. I started to cry and hammer on the bars like a maniac, a caged monkey, and I screamed:

'Captain Durán! Monica! Marcos!'

In the hours that passed while I was locked in the cell on my own I felt an anxiety that I have never experienced before or since and I couldn't tell you how long it was before they took me out of there. When they did, they took me to Captain Durán's office and I went from experiencing the worst situation a mother can have to one that was so adorable and sweet when I saw that huge man holding Monica and cooing at her. I started crying then, this time tears of happiness, and I felt completely safe.

They gave me a sandwich, took my passport and all my documents and asked me if I wanted to go back to the United States. I began to think that perhaps there wasn't such a predetermined plan for me in Venezuela as I had thought and in fact that those men didn't know what to do with me. I explained that I urgently needed some milk for my daughter and somewhere to sleep and they took me to a lovely suite at the

Hotel Ávila. Just as I had at the prison and on the way to the hotel, I insisted that I needed to see Marcos but they only answered with an evasive 'tomorrow, tomorrow'. Later, I found out that I had only been a few cells away from him and that the guards in that prison who looked after the former dictator were specially selected because of their hatred for him. They were relatives of prisoners who had been tortured under his regime.

Once at the hotel, they got some milk for me and a cot and they also brought fruit and flowers to the room where a guard was posted outside. They also left me a newspaper with my photograph on the front page under the title *'Arrested in Caracas — the lover and the daughter of Marcos Pérez Jiménez'*. Everything seemed strange but I don't really know why I wasn't frightened and I slept well that night. When I woke the next morning, Captain Durán came back to the hotel with four other officials and they took me to the Miraflores Palace where they told me they just wanted to talk to me. After walking along a marble corridor, we went into a large room with a huge table which was full of uniformed military personnel. I greeted them and they answered me very politely I still didn't feel frightened.

Sitting in the middle on one side of the enormous table, and under the intense scrutiny of the military personnel and of Simón Bolívar, one of several famous Venezuelans whose portraits adorned the walls, I started to answer a battery of questions beginning with why I had travelled to Caracas. I answered as I had so many times before: that I had come to see Marcos. I didn't need to explain anything else because I had Monica in my arms and her presence said it all: she looked like her father with features that evidently came from the native blood which ran through her veins.

The interrogation also referred to Cuba as well and they asked me if I had come to Caracas to start a revolution, if I was trying to bring Fidel's ideas to the country . . . Obviously they knew about my relationship with him but I reassured them, answering that I had no political intentions. They must have known something about my work with Fiorini and Operation 40 as well because they asked me whether I had transported arms to Venezuela. I replied with a definitive 'no'. I tried to explain to them that my daughter was now my life and that my more controversial deeds were now a thing of the past.

After a long session of questions and

answers, they told me I had to sign a document promising not to try to see Pérez Jiménez again. Just that, they explained to me. They would return my passport to me and I would be free to remain in Venezuela or return to the United States. They saw me as a dilemma for which there was no solution that was either logical or appealing. The only reason I had for being in the country was to see Marcos, to speak with him, explain to him how Walters had betrayed us and try to find a solution or a way forward. If I signed this agreement, it would be impossible and, although I could stay, I would have nothing to do there. I didn't know anyone there either and had no means of maintaining myself as mama had only given me a little extra money apart from the cost of the plane ticket. If I signed, it would give the green light to go back to the United States where someone was still threatening me, I didn't have any work and I didn't want to depend on my family. I could not see a future. In fact, I didn't want to go back. Anyway, without knowing what to do next, I signed.

Sightseeing in Venezuela
They had my promise that I wouldn't try to see Marcos again, but they didn't return my

passport to me immediately. They took me to the Hotel Ávila again. At five o'clock in the morning the following day they came to get me and, as a solution to my lack of immediate plans, they told me that they were going to take me and my child 'sightseeing'. We went to a military airport and boarded a small light aircraft belonging to SIFA which had just four seats. I had no idea where we were going. When I asked the pilot, who introduced himself as Pedro Fernández, he said:

'You'll see.'

The idea that the military would take me sightseeing seemed strange to me and I thought that perhaps they didn't trust me when I said that I wouldn't try to see Marcos again, that perhaps they wanted to keep me under control, that perhaps they wanted to hide me — although from whom? As it was impossible to get answers to my questions, I chose to give in to the pleasure of discovering the dramatic beauty of the country from the air. My proud Venezuelan lover had always described its natural beauty with enthusiasm. Just after flying over the Orinoco River, we landed and I found myself in Ciudad Bolívar, some 600 kilometres from Caracas. I found out later that they called it the last gateway to civilisation before the rainforest to the south started to take over everything like a dictatorial queen.

A car was waiting for us. It took us to a pretty colonial-style house surrounded by vegetation and a garden that was a little oasis. An older man and a woman picked up my bag and took me to a room on an upper floor. Pedro left me there and said that he had to go and get some fuel. I had no reason not to believe him and I didn't ask when he would come back or anything else but he didn't return the next day, nor the day after that, nor the day after that . . . When I asked my hosts about him, they told me that he always did the same thing and that he would return at some point. So I let myself be carried along again and while I waited for his return I fell into a pleasant routine.

I had breakfast every day with the lady of the house who was sweet and friendly. I started to help her in the garden and those days of working with the earth instilled a love of gardening in me that I have never abandoned. I loved seeing the plants and flowers grow. The lady also taught me to cook and I learned everything, from peeling garlic to how to handle tropical foods like cassava or avocado and how to prepare typical dishes like corn tortilla. Monica, mean-

207

while, spent her days playing and learned a few Spanish words and I enjoyed watching her and felt that, for once, we were living free from threat and stress. The house didn't have a telephone so I couldn't call mama to tell her that I was all right and safe there and I felt some uncertainty, of course, but I didn't think about it too much. I had decided not to miss out on anything in the first opportunity I had had for a long time to live a comfortable and peaceful life, without any worries, even though I was conscious that I was living on borrowed time there.

I couldn't say exactly how much time went by there but it was at least several weeks before Pedro the pilot returned without any warning, exactly as they had said he would. Without giving me any explanations as to why he hadn't returned before, he made me pack my case and say goodbye to our hosts. I cried a lot when I said goodbye to those wonderful people who had been so good to my daughter and me and who had offered us the security and peace that we needed. We boarded the small light aircraft again with Pedro, who was ac-companied by a co-pilot, and set off again without knowing our destination nor who was making the decisions about our stay in the country. All they said to me was that they were going to show me Venezuela.

'Don't Smile or They'll Eat Us Alive'

During the flight, the countryside appeared much greener and more dramatic than it had when we had travelled from Caracas to Ciudad Bolívar. Mountains appeared out of nowhere and I was amazed by them, although I was also worried about Pedro's flying because, without any warning, he would descend sharply and fly dangerously low or show off his skills at the controls with manoeuvres and turns that I felt were completely unnecessary and frightened Monica. We were in the air for longer than our first flight together when suddenly I heard a noise. I thought the wheels had been lowered for landing but either Pedro or his co-pilot said that someone was throwing something at us, which turned out to be arrows. I looked down and saw tiny figures like ants. As Pedro descended, the picture became clearer. They were dark-skinned people and at first I could have sworn that they were wearing red hats but then I realised they had red paint on their heads. I also saw some naked children running towards the adults. I asked who they were and Pedro told me they were Indians.

209

'They're ugly brutes and will try to eat us. When we land, don't smile or they'll eat us alive,' he advised. He was a sadist.

I could see a clearing among the vegetation and I soon realised that we were going to try to land there. It looked dangerous to me because it was such a small space and I also thought that Pedro should have been experienced enough to know that. Meanwhile, he kept putting the fear of God into me, telling me that some miners had been through there looking for gold but that there were none of them left because the Indians had eaten them.

Despite his macabre commentary, I banished my fears and felt a certain relief when we landed safely. Once the door was open, I saw a group of naked children running towards the plane. This was my first introduction to a tribe I later learned were Yanomami Indians and, perhaps because the children were the first direct contact I had with this completely unknown world, I wasn't afraid. Rather, I felt fortunate to have come to such a remote and isolated place and to have the opportunity to meet people whose contact with other human beings had clearly been minimal.

We stepped down from the plane and I began walking towards a hut, a rudimentary building made from four pieces of wood and a rickety roof which I noticed served as some sort of bar as there were a few bottles lying around. With Pedro's words ringing in my ears, I put on a serious face and didn't smile but my little Monica broke the ice and immediately started to play and laugh with the Yanomami children. Pedro took my Pan Am bag out of the plane and another little bag of nappies and things for Monica that I had bought in a pharmacy in Ciudad Bolívar and then walked back to the plane. I thought he was going to sit and wait for us. Then he said,

'See you later.'

At first, I didn't understand. Or at least I couldn't believe what I was hearing. I started to say that the place seemed very interesting but my daughter and I were leaving with him. He didn't let me finish.

'I'll be back.'

At that moment I was truly frightened. It wasn't the same as leaving me at the house in Ciudad Bolívar when he told me he was going to get fuel. He didn't even bother to give me an excuse this time. He just offered that 'I'll be back' that was so impossible to take in or get my head round. I grabbed Monica and the bags and started towards the plane. I tried to push past him to get on board but he pushed me back, saying no. I didn't have the strength to stay on my feet. I felt defeated and burst into tears and my daughter sank down when she heard me cry. When I saw Pedro step up into the plane, I tried to get on board again but the co-pilot held the door shut from the inside, stopping me opening it. Crying and falling further into the pit of despair with every passing moment, I begged and implored. I was terrified and unable to think clearly. Everything told me that I needed to get on that plane and go back with them to Ciudad Bolívar, or wherever they were flying to. If I didn't, I would be trapped. I couldn't get out of there on my own.

The engines roared into life and I was forced to step back from the plane with my daughter. I couldn't stop crying, feeling more terrified with every passing second. Then I had a moment of clarity and I realised that someone wanted to get rid of me, leave me abandoned there to die. No one I knew had the remotest idea where I was. The only thing they did know was that I had flown to Caracas but I hadn't told anyone that I had gone to Ciudad Bolívar and absolutely no one would have known that I had arrived in the rainforest which, with every passing second, was becoming a graveyard for me.

A sense of desperation that I had never before experienced flooded through me. Nothing compared to it, not even my time at Bergen-Belsen. In all the difficult situations I had been in up to then there had always been a chink that allowed a ray of hope through, a gap that allowed me to think about an exit, a way of escaping or a way of surviving. However, this was different. I felt completely abandoned.

The plane took off and I could only watch it through tears. As it became smaller and smaller, my sense of disbelief grew. My life was disappearing with that plane, flying over the rainforest. It was pure horror.

I was lost. I sat down and stayed still. I didn't know where to go and for a moment I thought that the pilot was playing one of his macabre and sadistic jokes on me. I thought he would turn around and come back for us but I waited and waited and heard nothing, just insects, monkeys and children playing. I only had what I was wearing and whatever was in my bags — some blue jeans, sports shoes, a bib and the products from the pharmacy in Ciudad Bolívar. Monica had arrived wearing little leather trousers and white booties and, when I looked at her, the Yanomami children

213

had taken everything off her.

The adults started to approach me, the men wearing boxer shorts and the women a little cord, a nakedness that I barely even noticed. They didn't smile or do anything to make me feel better either but I think they understood that I had been abandoned there. A woman approached me and helped me up while others nodded their heads. They took me to another rudimentary building below the one by the river with its completely brown water. The men were lying in hammocks. One of the women tended the fire beside which another woman was skinning a monkey and burning the hair from the pelt which stank. Others peeled cassava, green bananas and fruit. They talked among themselves and, between bouts of crying, I tried in vain to communicate with them. All my efforts were useless but something inside me began to tell me that, one way or another, everything was all right and that these people didn't seem to be like the image of savage monsters that Pedro had tried to plant in my head to frighten me. I don't know how or why but I knew that they weren't going to do me any harm.

Night was falling. My mind went blank but, in contrast, there was no silence around me. That first night I discovered that the noise of the rainforest is deafening, incessant, but despite the savage, constant noise and the anxiety, the terrifying anxiety, I was so exhausted that I dropped to the ground and fell asleep. By gesturing they had offered me a hammock. I had refused it and lay on the floor on some leaves.

A Home in the Rainforest

I opened my eyes before the sun came up, woken by the noise of the early rising Yanomami going about their morning activities. The women, for example, were preparing a fire. Anxiety also awoke me. I kept looking at the sky, hoping against hope that the plane would reappear. I made signs to the Yanomami but I wasn't communicating successfully and I was going round in circles without knowing who to talk to and how. I panic when I see snakes and I was frightened by everything that moved. It was full of bugs and insects that started to bother me. Smothered by an intensely sticky and humid heat that made me sweat all the time and without even the slightest breeze, I tried to find some refuge, sitting on a rock by the river where I was overcome by great sadness and anxiety. I felt condemned and alone, perplexed and confused, caught in a snare, and I didn't know if it had been set by Walters or the CIA. I hardly ate anything that day, just a few roots, a small, brown banana they gave me and a little bit of fish.

It took three or four days for me to become sick. My stomach started to hurt and I had diarrhoea, nausea and very intense headaches. I was both freezing and absolutely roasting and I was trembling continually and couldn't stand up. These awful sensations were a relief on the one hand because I was so focused on the pain that I stopped thinking about how to get out of there. A Yanomami woman kept me alive by making me put some leaves in my mouth which I chewed. They were bitter but I got used to chewing them and they made me feel better. They were like magic. When I put them in my mouth and started to chew, it only took a few minutes for the pain to evaporate. Little by little, with the help of the leaves, I began to feel alive again and I started to eat. I owe my life to those people whom Pedro had described as uncivilised and savage.

I had lost a lot of weight but, when I recovered my strength, I started to help with the women's activities. We collected wood, cut it, made a fire and cooked while the men stayed in their hammocks, often drunk on the alcohol they fermented. I overcame my revulsion and began to eat monkey and snake meat and some white beans that we put in the fire on sticks. I also tried to imitate the women in the work they did with their hands, at which they were very skilled. They took leaves and, by tearing them with a sharpened instrument, they made cords and wove baskets with them at an incredible speed. What I could never work out is how they identified the leaves with medicinal properties. They knew them all. When I came back with scratches or bites, they went into the rainforest and came back with some leaves to prepare a paste that made sure that my wounds didn't become infected and healed and, as well as that, they helped to stop me being stung.

At the beginning I had lived under a huge tree but when the rains and storms arrived it didn't provide enough protection. I must have made them feel sorry for me or inspired compassion as they built me a kind of cabin in a corner below the main hut, a long building where they lived and met together.

That was my life and my greatest satisfaction was that I could see Monica growing up happy and free. She was completely feral and ran around barefoot, playing all day with the Yanomami children. She learned to fish with arrows like the other children. She played games in which they raced large insects. She had a monkey as a pet. She was perfectly integrated as one of them and, watching her, it made me realise that children are children and there is no hatred or racism in their world, something that we adults would do well to remember. Sometimes, as well, when I saw her with the other children I thought about her native blood and I began to think that her DNA was so strong that it had ensured our destiny was to bring her back to her roots.

The rainforest had become my home and I saw a different world, full of an immense variety of plants and leaves, a world of seven orchids which reminded me of the days when Marcos talked to me about the national flower of Venezuela. I learned to have faith in knowledge about every tree, every plant, every drop of water to keep me alive and free of pain. The children taught me useful lessons such as how to make a trail with branches when I went into the rainforest so that I knew the way back. My own daughter taught me so much there. She had no fear.

I also had a suitor. His name was Catchu. He wasn't very tall, about 1.70 metres, with very dark skin and big round eyes that were also dark. At the beginning, he just followed me and looked at me. Then, through gestures, he told me that he was going to make me a hammock, the most important present you can give in that community, which was a kind of proposal of marriage. I didn't love him or want to marry him but I was grateful for his company and his attention. The rest of the community knew that I liked him and they allowed him to flirt with me and left us alone sometimes. He came up to me and stroked my arm or hand gently, always tenderly, never aggressively or forcefully like too many men were accustomed to do in a world that was supposedly civilised.

It was a pleasant life that, to a certain extent, I was happy with and at least I had my daughter with me. I started to think that perhaps that was our destiny. I still wanted to leave but passing time was my enemy and the sky didn't offer any answers. Little by little, I was giving up and I stopped looking upwards. I didn't pray because I didn't know how to pray or to whom. Deep within me, I had never given up hope that they would come back to find me and I kept hoping that someone would remember us, that someone would recognise their guilt and feel sorry for the woman and child abandoned in the rainforest . . . However, I didn't really hold out much hope of that; I didn't trust anyone. If I had any hope at all, it was in Marcos. I thought he would be able to get us out of there, that he would rescue us, or if not his lover then at least his daughter. I just had to hope that he was out of prison.

Instead of pinning my hopes on him, I should have known better and thought of the one person who had always cared about me my entire life: mama. It was she who made the effort to find us after several months without any news from me. First she sent money as cheques in my name for me to collect in Caracas and, when I didn't do that, she knew that we weren't in the capital, the only place that she was sure we had been. Then she got in touch with Walters and the CIA, demanding to know where we were and insisting they move heaven and earth so that someone would give her some clues or an explanation about her daughter and granddaughter. No one replied but mama finally found a contact — I never knew who it was — who made some enquiries and found me. So, thanks to her, one day a small aircraft appeared in the middle of the rainforest. It wasn't the SIFA plane that I had been dreaming of but one from the Red Cross.

When I saw it approaching I fell to my knees in the place that had been my home for months, perhaps eight or nine, and I cried until I could cry no more. I was so happy! The Yanomami had become my family and I didn't want to leave them and I was even more frightened thinking about what I was returning to after living in the rainforest. However, I also knew that I had to get on the plane. I looked terrible, full of parasites and covered in bites and I had dysentery. I weighed about forty kilos and I stank. Monica had her own scars. We had to leave.

I started to hug the men, women and children who had been our saviours and our friends and, with tears in my eyes, I said goodbye to them. It made my heart bleed, more than anything when it was time to say goodbye to the old woman who had looked after me when I became ill by giving me her leaves and herbs and made me feel so alive during my time there. They stroked my face with a heartfelt sadness. Catchu stayed to one side, looking at the ground, over-whelmed by sadness, and I think he felt rejected. He had just finished the hammock for me.

Two of the men who had just arrived accompanied Monica and I to the small plane and, when we got in, I knew I was safe and that I was going to get out of there; I had survived once again.

They gave us bottled water on the flight and some tablets that they told me were for malaria and made me feel very sleepy. The men carried on talking and I remember them saying something about 'your mother' and mentioning an 'investigation' but I wasn't conscious or coherent enough to understand much. It was as if my whole being was giving up after having fought to stay alive. I collapsed.

We arrived at Caracas airport and boarded another flight to Florida, I don't remember if we went to Key West or Miami. As soon as we landed, they took us to hospital where we had numerous tests, after which they told me that I had had malaria and that Monica had an infection from a bite. For a while afterwards her nose became periodically inflamed and even today she has a mark which is a vestige of that part of her childhood that she spent in the rainforest.

'It's Not so Easy'

I called Carlos Pulido, the old colonel who was a friend of Marcos, from the hospital and I cried when I told him all that had happened to me. He, his wife and his two daughters came to see me in the hospital as did the captain who had taken Marcos and me several times to Soldier Key to the *Flor Mar,* the ten-metre-long boat that Pérez Jiménez had named in honour of his wife. The one person who didn't come was mama as she was in New Jersey but we spoke on the phone.

'It's a miracle that you're alive. Why do you put your life at risk like that?' she rebuked me.

'I didn't want to, mama . . .' I replied with a knot in my stomach.

'Why don't you use your head?'

'It's not so easy . . .'

'Why don't you grow up? Thank God you're alive but you would never have got out if I hadn't called *the boys.'*

I couldn't say anything else and I just cried. I cried because I knew that mama was right and, if it hadn't been for her, perhaps I would have died in the rainforest, abandoned to the elements by God knows who. Perhaps it was someone who thought I was a problem or likely to cause an international incident and they wanted me to disappear or die. I cried because it was truly a miracle that my daughter and I were alive. I cried because I had risked not only my own life but the life of my baby as well. I cried because I was sure that I had to find another ship to steer but I didn't even know where that was. I cried and cried because everything that had happened had been in vain. I had failed in the one thing I wanted to do: to see Marcos.

CHAPTER 7
MAFIA GIRL AND SPY IN NEW YORK

The Pulido family, who had looked after me since the accident, became my hosts and guardians again for almost a month after my return from the rainforest. Little by little, I was readjusting to a 'civilised' life in which everything surprised me, from car horns to traffic lights to telephones. I was back in Miami, a city with too much history for me, too much of a past, too many people I knew and too many setbacks. I was anxious to be, as so many times before, anonymous, just Monica's mother, and this wasn't a good place to do that.

So I decided to go back to Fort Lee with my mother, who was still living at 206 Wilson Avenue, and I tried to live a normal life. I saw my brothers, I assisted Philip at his concerts and looked for a job, trying to be just another citizen. I aspired to be, definitively, an 'ordinary' woman but, as usual, it wasn't going to be as easy as I thought.

I constantly met people whom it would have been better to avoid, like Charlie *The Blade* Tourine, a member of the Italian Mafia, linked with the Genovese family and whose nickname alluded to the switchblade he used with skill when confronting other gangsters or debtors who didn't pay. He was a very nice man who I had known from my maritime adventures: he worked for Eddie Flynn, the head of the ports in New York, and they both travelled on *papa*'s ships. He was both a skilled diplomat and a born survivor and sometimes he organised dinners for the Mafia port staff and also for the AFL-CIO syndicate, and maintained excellent relations with these corrupt worlds which were bound by *omertà,* the code of silence, where it was much more convenient to get along with them well rather than so-so or badly. 'Uncle Charlie' had also been one of Santo Trafficante's men in Havana and managed the San Souci club for him in the Hotel Capri.

Sicilian by birth, Uncle Charlie lived in a luxurious apartment at 40 Central Park South and in those days when they began to organise junkets — travel packages so that people could gamble outside the casino — he was *capo dei capi,* controlling those who took gamblers to Paradise Island in the

Bahamas. While he was on one of those trips he asked me if I would stay at his house and look after the money he had there so, on those occasions, I told mama that I was going to babysit a small fortune which was kept in shoeboxes and I went with Monica to that luxury refuge in 'the lungs' of Manhattan. Uncle Charlie paid me for the time he was away. On a few occasions he took me and my daughter with him and I spent a whole month on Paradise Island living like a queen with absolutely everything paid for, from the suite to the boat trips, going into the most exclusive clubs and evening shows.

I didn't have sexual relations with Uncle Charlie. He was a womaniser and had been married six times but he wasn't my type and he didn't try it on either. He was a very lonely man who had spent too much time in prison and wanted someone to be close to him, someone to hold. However, he wasn't looking for sex — at least not with me.

Even with everything he made available to me, I was bored. As he was determined that I should put my past — turbulent, shadowy and full of risks — behind me and he didn't want me to go back to Miami under any circumstances, he converted his apartment in Central Park to create a room for Monica which he filled with all the things money could buy to look after and entertain a little girl. I once joked about all the money he had and, half in jest, I asked if he printed it himself. He didn't find it funny and, visibly annoyed, he said:

'Never, ever, touch counterfeit money.'

Humberto, My Gay Husband

I tried hard to be a respectable citizen and an ordinary woman and, thanks to Uncle Charlie, I managed to get a job as a receptionist at the Statler Hilton, the same hotel in which I had stayed with Fidel when I had visited New York in April 1959. I don't know how the devil I managed to keep the job for almost a month because I didn't have any education or experience but I did it and, while I was there, I met a Cuban, Humberto Núñez Webster, a businessman who always carried a briefcase and who came constantly to reception to talk to me even though I wasn't a guest at the hotel. Humberto was extremely attractive. He had the most beautiful face I had ever seen and I liked him very much and went out with him a couple of times. Soon after, he asked me if I would marry him. Although marriage wasn't in my plans, on one occasion after I had had an argument with mama I was furious and went with Humberto to Lower Manhattan where they carried out civil marriages and so I became Mrs Marita Webster.

At first we lived with my mother and then moved into Philip's apartment as he was on a world tour. One day while we were there I opened Humberto's briefcase and jewellery, ID in different names, a gun, a set of skeleton keys and other hardware fell out, all of which clearly showed that his 'business' was theft. When I confronted him and asked him to explain it to me, he said it wasn't necessary and I didn't know what I was talking about. I realised then that it was all a deception and that I didn't really know who this man was, what he did or why he had been so keen to marry me. He eventually confessed that he was homosexual and didn't even like women. I had always thought that his promise to look after me was really a cover to get money from Marcos Pérez Jiménez.

After confessing that he was homosexual, and I had found out about his occupation and deceptions, it was clear that we couldn't stay together but, even so, he gave me the security of a permanent address and some money and he asked me to fetch a camera from a shop on 8th Avenue in Lower Manhattan. I went there and picked up the camera but as I left two detectives from 28th Precinct, who were based in Spanish Harlem but were part of a city-wide operation dealing with theft, stopped me, saw what I was carrying and told me that the camera was stolen. I was frightened but I was able to convince the officers that I had been sent by my husband. More importantly, I succeeded in doing something else: in order to get Humberto put away, I started to collaborate with one of the detectives, John Justy.

A couple of weeks later I was dating J.J., my husband was in Sing Sing, the maximum security prison in the north of New York state, and my new boyfriend offered to give evidence to get the marriage with Humberto annulled.

Mafia Girl and Disco Kid

I loved J.J. and I should have run away with him and become his wife. The problem was that he drank a lot, too much. He was an alcoholic and I couldn't handle it. Not only that, my relationship with him wasn't the only one I had at that time. During the day I divided my time between Uncle Charlie's house and mama's house as she had moved from New Jersey to New York and now lived in the Upper East Side at 305 East 86th Street. I visited people like Eddie Flynn, the head of the New York ports, and I did nothing useful. By contrast, my nights were very busy and I started going out constantly, particularly with a friend, Kathy, a madam of Cherokee blood who ran one of the biggest escort agencies in the city and I became a 'Mafia girl' and 'disco kid'.

Then I went through a very sad chapter in my life. In 1966 we knew that *papa* was very ill in Germany. He had been suffering from liver cancer for some time but his condition started to deteriorate very quickly and, although my brother Joe was able to be with him, mama and I didn't get there in time. We went by sea but the bad news arrived before we docked. *Papa* had died. My mother fell into a deep depression and I experienced a profound sadness. We tried to comfort each other saying that his death had caught us while we were en route but I hated myself for not having got there in time to say goodbye to him. JoJo sent us lots of photographs of the funeral, which was very well attended; flags were flown at half-mast and that really broke my heart. I went to see all the people who had known *papa* in New York to break the news and remember him with them but I couldn't go anywhere near the port.

I went through a period of mourning. However, before long my life went back to being all about one thing: partying. I seemed to have no direction. I went to all the fashionable places and danced all night and, although I didn't use drugs, I drank as many Cuba Libre cocktails and vodka and oranges as I could. It was as if I wanted to make up for all the partying I had missed, to forget all the ups and down of the past. I was always out till four or five in the morning and ended up at parties at illegal 'after hours' places or at private houses. I flirted continually, mostly with Mafia people, because a friend of mine called Charlene was a lover of Stevie Gallo, a nephew of the three Gallo brothers, prominent members of the Colombo family, one of the five Mafia families in the Cosa Nostra in New York, and we moved in his circle.

Mama, who would stay overnight to look after Monica, was furious with me but I couldn't control myself, either going out or in my hectic love life where I had a multitude of boyfriends, often men I used purely for my own satisfaction and who had no hold on my heart. We jokingly called it 'fuck and run'. I wanted to meet a good man but you usually didn't find them in bars, clubs or 'after hours' places. They were just toys and everyone played around with everyone else. I was young and beautiful and I wanted to be desired. Once I'd had a man I lost interest in him. I know it wasn't a nice game but it kept me entertained for a while, particularly with the Mafiosi. I went out with some middle-order guys and also with some who were further up in the family hierarchy, such as Tommy *Tea Balls* Mancuso or one of the Gallos who would die years later in prison but was sweet and adorable to me, one of my favourite lovers.

The Mata Hari of the Caribbean

It was a different time then from today. I connected with everyone and, although it might seem a contradiction, I felt safe with the Mafia. I was happy and relaxed for the first time in my life. I was treated well and that was mainly because the word was out about what I had done in Cuba which came from people imprisoned by Fidel. That earned me the affectionate nickname of 'the Mata Hari of the Caribbean' which they still use today. They joked about it often, saying that without me there couldn't be a party. I lived on the gratitude as well and they also looked after me because they considered me trustworthy and they knew I could keep a secret. I understood how it all worked, from respecting Sunday, a family day the Italians spent with their wives and children, to doing what was expected of a Mafia girlfriend: to be beautiful and ready to go out when required and when a car was sent to collect me. In exchange, they were gallant and respectful. My mother was horrified by the people I was mixing with and sometimes asked me if I realised who I was going out with. But they were even sweet to her. They would call her *mamma* and often filled her house with flowers, candy and presents from televisions to coffee or pistachio nuts which might be part of lorry cargoes they had stolen. We even had to get a new refrigerator for all the meat they gave us.

I was familiar with the unwritten rules such as how grassing to the police was a death sentence, never to associate with them and never say or do anything that would incriminate anyone. If they ended up in prison, you demonstrated your loyalty to them, writing letters or sending parcels. I also knew how to win their confidence in more serious matters. They could shoot someone in front of you and you simply looked the other way and left. You never repeated anything you had heard and you didn't listen to conversations that had nothing to do with you. To survive, I had only to apply the mantra that had already been hammered into me in our basement during the war in Germany: don't speak, don't think, don't breathe.

More Honourable than the CIA

The Mafia had a code that inspired a lot more confidence in me than the one used by the CIA who had taught me to lie rather than tell the truth. The godfathers were true gentlemen you could trust, people for whom their word was their bond and where there was more respect and less duplicity than in the Agency.

I should have just gone out with Italian Mafiosi but, while at a disco one day I met Edward *Eddie* Levy, a heavyweight in the Kosher Nostra, the Jewish Mafia. He was married, though that didn't stop us becoming lovers. I had a fabulous, lasting relationship with him, full of love. In spite of the fact that the Italian Mafia weren't entirely happy about my relationship with someone from the Kosher Nostra, they respected it and Eddie loved me and looked after me. As well as showering me with presents such as a $36,000 diamond ring, he tried, as

Uncle Charlie had, to change my life and make it more enjoyable, a promise that he demonstrated by paying for a year's course at the Eastern School for Physicians, a centre for training medical assistants, which I kept starting and stopping. Perseverance in my studies, never one of my strengths, was even weaker at this time.

It was also Eddie who paid for my ticket to Madrid to go and see Marcos. In August 1968 Venezuela released Pérez Jiménez from prison and he had chosen Spain as his place of exile. Although I had bombarded him with letters for the five years he had been in prison, I never knew if they reached him and never received an answer, and it was only after he was freed that I managed to speak to him by telephone when he was staying in a hotel in Madrid. When I got through to Marcos, it opened the floodgates to a torrent of sorrows, the story of our abandonment in the rainforest, memories of the wicked betrayal by Walters . . . Monica took the telephone and was able to speak to her *papi* for the first time and we left it that we would go to Madrid to see him. It was an emotional and tender conversation. Mama recorded it but someone, we never knew exactly who, how, or when, stole the tape. Perhaps it was the CIA.

I left Monica with mama and, with the ticket paid for by Eddie, I flew to Spain and stayed at the Intercontinental Hotel in Madrid, very close to where Marcos was. Without further ado I spoke to him by telephone again and we made plans to meet the next day. Happy and satisfied, I went down to the shop in the hotel to buy one of those bolero jackets with tassels which were fashionable then. I was finally going to see Marcos again. I slept well, went down to breakfast and the last thing on my mind was that someone, once again, would make sure that nothing would go to plan. They must have put something in my food because I spent hours and hours asleep at the hotel, an enforced sleep that knocked me out for two days. When I recovered, I realised what had happened and I tried to call Marcos but there was no response from the hotel and I telephoned my mother to tell her that they had followed me and that someone was doing something to me. I didn't know who was behind it all, but it was probably Marcos's wife who hated me and hated Monica, or someone linked to her, although it had also crossed my mind that the attack could be the work of someone in the US government.

Whoever it was they were sending me a

message and one that was impossible to misinterpret: I had to leave. I didn't want to live my life in fear again, to feel insecure and uncertain and, even more, I didn't want my daughter to suffer. It wasn't worth risking my life again and leaving Monica without a mother so I boarded a plane and returned to the United States, disappointed, disillusioned and frustrated. When I arrived, Frankie Gio, another of my boyfriends who had friends in the Mafia and who appeared in *The Godfather* films, warned me not to try to see Marcos again because, if I did, someone was going to try to wipe me off the map.

Mark's Difficult Arrival

After the abortive trip, mama became my support again, my refuge and, as she had been when I first came back from Cuba, she was my door to collaboration with the federal authorities in the United States. Monica and I lived with her in her house on the Upper East Side, an apartment in a building which was looked after by a man named Louis Yurasits. My love life was quite busy but when Eddie decided to take his wife on a world cruise for several months I was angry with him and, almost as if in revenge, I started a relationship with Louis.

He and mama introduced me to Al Chestone, Uncle Al from then on, a man who I could only describe as having a style of his own. I found out later that he was an FBI agent and Louis, who appeared to be a superintendent, was spying for him. Uncle Al suggested that Louis and I team up. I was recruited and that was the beginning of a five-year posting with the Federal Bureau of Investigation.

The first requirement was to go through a period of training with the FBI but, aside from professional matters, Uncle Al, who was a fervent Catholic, was also worried about my personal life and wanted me to marry Louis. I was pregnant again and my new FBI godfather wanted the baby to have a name.

The birth of my second child, who arrived on 13 December 1969, was very difficult. I had placenta previa, a complication during pregnancy which concerns the growth of the placenta towards the lower part of the uterus and covers the neck of the womb, impeding the baby's exit during birth. I also had pre-eclampsia and I had a minor heart attack. The baby arrived weighing almost five kilos and he was breach birth so they had to do an emergency caesarean section. I started to scream when I heard the doctors and nurses talking about acute foetal distress and I was terrified when I realised that my baby wasn't breathing after his birth. They were covering him with a white sheet but, luckily, the baby peed and we knew he had survived, although he had to spend a week in an incubator.

Fortunately, they had taken me to Columbus Hospital in Midtown which, in those days, had the best recovery record in the city. I could hear my mother crying in the room outside. Several of my lovers were with her, J.J., Frankie Gio, Tommy *Tea,* Eddie . . . I could hear them arguing about paternity, which made me feel great tenderness towards them. In fact, I baptised my baby, Mark Edward, in homage to Eddie who had lost a daughter to a brain tumour. He insisted that the baby, with red hair like him, was his but I knew it was Louis's. I had only to count the months that my Kosher Nostra lover had been out of the country on a cruise.

In those days it took three months to complete the birth certificate and that was the time it took to formally christen him Mark. Uncle Al managed to get the authorities to pay for a ticket for Louis to go to Mexico on one of the 'freedom flights', express transfers to a neighbouring country where you could get a divorce quicker than in the United States. I accompanied Louis on that trip. He was still married so we managed to get him a divorce from his previous wife and returned to New York where, in a civil ceremony, we became husband and wife on 28 February 1970. I had written Mark Edward Yurasits on the birth certificate. Soon he would acquire the nickname 'Beegie', a reminder of some Chinese lanterns in the shape of a bee that I had been given to put over the cot, the first sound we heard him utter.

Despite being sure of my son's paternity, it was hurtful to deny Eddie so I gave him free rein to act as the baby's father. He took Mark to one of the Mafia meeting places when he was just three or four months old and introduced him proudly as 'my boy'. In those days he also wanted to kill Louis who he hated and called him 'that Hungarian bastard' and even put $50,000 on the table to make him disappear from my life. My husband refused.

Different Types of Rats

Married and looking after our baby and Monica, Louis and I received our first mission from Uncle Al once our training was completed. At 250 East 87th Street, Glenwood Management was inaugurating a new building, a skyscraper comprising luxury apartments with a swimming pool on the top floor where the FBI intended to keep an eye on everything. Several families from United Nations diplomatic legations were moving in from the Soviet Union as well as countries within its orbit such as Bulgaria or Albania, and they rented the entire twenty-first floor. Before the tenants moved in, they bugged all the apartments and Louis and I were supposed to back this up by collecting all possible information. So we moved into a beautiful apartment in the building and we began work on our mission for which the FBI would pay me $500 a month, although it could be more, depending on various factors.

I didn't want to do the job and it was a question of rats. Of two kinds of rat. At the beginning of 1971 we had only been in the apartment a short time when one night Beegie, who was then thirteen months old, started to cry. It reignited my maternal fear that someone was trying to take my children away from me or harm them and I went to get my gun. When I approached the cot, I saw that my baby had blood around his mouth and, horrified, I realised he had gone to sleep with his bib on. Rats had smelled the milk, had got into the cot and had not only bitten through the teat of the bottle but my son's lip, too. The first thing I did was take him to the Emergency Department at the Metropolitan Hospital where he was admitted him and found to have developed a fever from the rat bite. One of the symptoms was that it paralysed his stomach and left him with consequences that still affect him today. When I went home, furious, I blamed Louis, fired a shot into the air conditioning unit and swore blind that I would sue the builders. Because of the hurry to build and rent the apartments to enable the espionage to take place, they had rushed part of the work and, among other things, hadn't closed the air vents properly. I had no doubt that that was how the rats had got in and attacked Mark.

Not long after, I was in the lift one day when a man approached me and stepped in just as the doors were closing, just like in the movies.

'What are you doing? Causing problems?' he spat in a menacing manner.

'Who are you?' I asked, a little tired.

'You will die very quickly if you don't stop meddling,' he said and he pushed the button for the top floor where the still unfinished swimming pool was located. When the door opened, the wild animal within me emerged, the same person capable of holding dozens of men at arm's length, soldiers with evil faces and the devil in their eyes, and I said:

'What are you going to do now? Get out of my way.'

He answered with the classic reply, 'do you know who you're talking to?' but it didn't scare me and I replied:

'Do *you* know who you're talking to? Stop playing games. Let's go back down.'

Later I found out his name, Gino, a thug who worked as 'muscle' for the Sicilian Mafia and someone whom the owners of the company had contracted to throw out tenants who paid low rents in brownstones or to burn buildings to make room for their skyscrapers. That contretemps in the lift was the first time I met him, although it would not be the last. In fact, Gino became another of my lovers.

The Science of Garbage

Despite the incidents with the rat and Gino, the mission went ahead. Some of the work I did, for example, was to go down to the room where the garbage was collected to recover letters or documents that the tenants might have thrown away, something that the Russians rarely did but what was there was thrown away mainly by the Albanians. I took the rubbish up to the apartment where one of the bathrooms had been converted to a kind of espionage office, with soundproofing and a large table over the toilet bowl, a lamp, markers and special tape. When I found documents that had been shredded I pieced them together like a jigsaw puzzle and delivered them in the mornings to Uncle Al who had to come in very early. Before taking the documents and giving me new tasks, he helped me look after Beegie and even changed his nappy while I took a shower.

I also carried out spying operations outside the building and I had to take down car registration numbers and make a note of people entering and leaving. The FBI also had an apartment on the other side of the street in the Mayflower apartments, to take photographs of visits, and they sometimes surprised me with how lax they were. Once I had to get Uncle Al to tell them not to light their cigarettes at night while they were on watch and taking photos because, despite the venetian blinds at the windows, I could see them perfectly.

Aside from work, I felt happy being married to Louis and I had a sense of security then I hadn't felt before and that I haven't experienced since. I felt protected and I also had a father for Beegie and a stepfather for Monica, although my daughter ended up moving in with my mother when she also took an apartment in a brownstone on 87th Street which was next to my building. Mama didn't like Louis much. She thought he was a brute, even though he was an engineer, and acted like a wicked mother-in-law, which he tolerated. I always thought that for her no one I was with would ever be good enough. Yet, for me, there was something very comfortable about life with Louis and I even gave up some of my lovers, at least for a while.

A Spy As Well As a Police Officer

In those years when the Cold War was in full swing there was no one side that wasn't under constant surveillance by the other and the Soviet tenants with whom Louis and I established good and friendly relationships, who filled the apartment with presents such as vodka and large tins of caviar, were extremely cautious. As they spent most of the day at the UN or in their consulates or missions, they spread their apartments with cables, flour or any other kind of dust so that they would know if anyone had entered, and that was how they detected intrusions a couple of times which they reported to the police. To avoid diplomatic incidents, they had to investigate the reports and that's how I got involved with the New York Police Department as an auxiliary, in a division which dealt with complaints received about criminal activity. I was responsible for answering calls so that when the Soviet mission telephoned to report someone entering one of their apartments it was me who took the call and I would organise the showpiece investigation that would calm the Soviets down by making it look as if the case was being looked into; in reality, it was being buried.

Those days were also the high point for the Black Liberation Army and we had some of their members in the building. Louis didn't want black tenants because he felt that having to watch them would interfere with the central mission which was to spy on the Soviets. For me, however, it wasn't a problem to broaden our horizons. One day I used Louis's master key to enter one of the apartments where I found a lot of literature relating to the movement which had risen just after the FBI had infiltrated the Black Panthers. I saw that there were also bullet shells in the apartment and I automatically put some of them in my pocket. When they were analysed, their markings showed that they had been fired from the same gun as the bullets used in the killing of two police officers, Joseph Piagentini and Waverly Jones, in an infamous assassination on 21 May 1971.

I had not only discovered an important clue to finding the murderers of the two police officers, but it represented the start of another affair for me in this world in which, not so long ago, I had moved like a fish in water, although lately I had been a relatively good girl: the world of lovers. As the case relating to the Black Liberation Army fell to the Organized Crime Division, Uncle Al arranged a meeting for me with one of the inspectors in that department. I had to meet him one day at 10 a.m. in Leo's Diner on East 86th Street. I had instructions to look for a large man with blue eyes who would be in plainclothes. When I arrived and saw him, the first thing I said was,

'I don't want to work for you. I'd rather make love.'

He tried to change the subject, asking me if I wanted tea, coffee, a doughnut or something for breakfast but he had set off something in me that was unstoppable and I insisted:

'I just want you.'

Captain Frank Xavier Smith, who, in those days of rampant police corruption, also worked for Internal Affairs, resisted my advances, but gave me his card and we parted. When I returned home, my husband knew at once that there was a problem. I couldn't get the man I had just met out of my head and I called him the following day.

'This is your invisible source, the one who didn't accept a cup of tea. I want to see you. It's about work,' I said.

I didn't really have any intention of working and I would say that he didn't either because he met me in a Marriott Hotel and that day saw the beginning of a relationship that lasted for the next fifteen years.

CHAPTER 8
FIORINI'S RETURN:
MY PERSONAL WATERGATE

I spent the next few years putting back
together the pieces of my life with as much
normality as was possible within the com-
plexity of the puzzle, and although I aspired
to be an ordinary person, I was one woman
and many different ones all at the same
time. I spied by day, worked with the police
at night and managed to balance family life
with that of my lovers. I loved Frank Smith,
I didn't want to hurt Eddie, I couldn't leave
Louis and I was working professionally with
Uncle Al. Mama's unhappiness with everything and each of my relationships was on
obstacle and my affairs had also damaged
my marriage with Louis who himself started
an affair with a woman in the building, an
infidelity I could obviously say nothing
about. But all that seemed trivial compared
to what was about to happen.

Under his mother's maiden name, Sturgis, Frank Fiorini was arrested on 17 June

1972 together with Virgilio Gonzáles, Eugenio Martínez, Bernard Barker and James McCord for entering the offices of the Democratic Party in the Watergate Building, Washington, DC, where they had gone to retrieve some badly installed microphones. In January the following year, 1973, they were sentenced, along with Gordon Liddy and Howard Hunt, the man who I had known as 'Eduardo' during my time in Florida.

I drove to Danbury State Penitentiary in Connecticut to try to see him but they told me he had been transferred to a prison in Washington, DC, so I went back to New York. Through Hank Messick, a journalist who had written about the Mafia and had published a biography of Meyer Lansky and was a friend of Louis, I got a number for Frank at the prison and I soon heard that lying, lousy voice again. The first thing I asked him was what exactly had happened to Alex Rorke because I was sure that he had the answer to his disappearance a decade earlier and that it damaged the US government and the CIA, Cuban exiles, the Mafia, Fidel and even Frank himself. But he didn't seem to be interested in talking about that. He wanted to know if I had any influence at all to get him out of there and, if I could help him to get out through someone in my circle, my Mafia friends or some other way.

'I can't help you. This isn't a theft from some armoury, it's much bigger than that. It's the White House!' I reminded him. 'Anyway, where were you when I needed your help dealing with Walters in Miami?'

Sturgis spent three months in prison and while he was there increasingly began to sense that he had been betrayed, a feeling matched only by a fury at being abandoned by the same authorities for whom he had worked for years. Meanwhile, the CIA tried to recruit me again. I received a visit to our building from John Effenito, an agent who wanted to let me work both with the FBI and return to work with 'the Firm' again. He suggested that I had to do it as a matter of national security, to collaborate in something to do with Watergate. His visits to the building put my mission in danger so I told Uncle Al who stopped Effenito one day in the lobby of the building when he came to see me and told him that I worked for them now and managed to get him to leave me in peace.

The United States, a Pandora's Box

Watergate was a wave more powerful than anything else at the time. It was a tsunami that really shook the United States, a country which, after the Kennedy assassinations and this scandal and the subsequent collapse of the Nixon administration, had opened the lid on a veritable Pandora's Box.

Much has been said about that being the time when the country lost its innocence and it is true that it would have been impossible to contain it once the numerous misdemeanours of the CIA and FBI started to come out into the open, such as links with the Mafia, which reached the highest echelons of government, and possible state-sponsored conspiracies to assassinate foreign leaders, from Fidel in Cuba to Patrice Lumumba in the Congo or Rafael Trujillo in the Dominican Republic. Everything was very messy, although it began to provide irrefutable evidence, and made the notion more plausible, that nothing in the assassination of JFK had been as they had described so far. In those days investigations proliferated such as the so-called Rockefeller Commission which, in 1975, tried to shine a light on certain aspects of the assassination. In 1975, there was also an investigation undertaken by the Church

253

Committee in the Senate which dedicated one of its reports to outlining the plan by CIA Director Allen Dulles, which was approved by Eisenhower, to use the Sicilian Mafia in his plans to kill Fidel.

For the forces working in the shadows at that time, Sturgis had to be one of their very worst nightmares. He was a man with too much to say and a lot to be silent about and accustomed to acting exactly as he wished, something that made him as unpredictable as he was dangerous, especially after he been imprisoned and, to his mind, betrayed. I could certainly testify that he continued to be selfish, driven only by his own interest, and was a true soldier of fortune. When he came up with a strategy that would enable him to get revenge as well as make money, he saw me as a pawn that he didn't mind sacrificing.

Exposed

One day, in May or June 1975, Manny Rodríguez, the manager of our building, told me that a journalist had been looking for Marita Lorenz, although in those days I was known as Mrs Yurasits. When I contacted the reporter, Paul Meskil, I understood that he had the whole story from Sturgis, that he had included me in his story and he had even managed to find a photo of me with Fidel. I spoke with Frank and told him indignantly that I was in the middle of an operation spying on the Soviets and that he was putting that in danger. When I asked him what he was playing at and what the devil he was saying about me to the press, he replied sarcastically,

'Touché. You failed to kill Fidel and I told you that it would come back to haunt you.'

He had set the trap but I fell into it by myself and I was my own worst enemy because, when I got in touch with Meskil again, I tried to worm out of him what he knew. Although I only confirmed details to him that Sturgis had already told, he took advantage of our chat to say that I had given him an interview. Days later, on Sunday 20 April 1975, an article appeared in a series dubbed *'Secrets of the CIA'* under the heading *'The Mata Hari who deceived Castro'*, along with my photo and my story. When I saw the paper in a kiosk, I knew my downfall was imminent. The first thing that came into my head was what Frank Smith, my lover in the police, would think. Then I thought about Louis, although he knew the basic details about my life. I went back home with a copy of the paper, put it on the table and told my husband who didn't seem particularly bothered.

'We're finished. Don't you understand what this means? The operation is over. Everyone in the apartment is going to know who I am.'

I wasn't wrong and everything did indeed fall apart. Once my story and discoveries about my past and my identity were exposed, the Soviet tenants moved to another building in Riverdale.

Although our divorce wasn't finalised until 22 January 1976, Louis and I split up and he replaced me very quickly with a topless dancer from a bar on Second Avenue who moved in with him. She got everything: the furniture, the clothes and my husband. The break-up hurt me a lot and I regret it even now because I know it was a mistake. I should have stayed with that man who I loved, in my own way, and with whom I had a good life which was, to a certain extent, quiet. I never meant to do him any harm. His departure was also very traumatic for little Mark although Louis's later rejection of his son, his miserable attitude and his complete neglect, leaving us without any financial support or maintenance and not even anything for his education, transformed the pain into contempt.

Finished

While things were falling apart, as I was driving along East River Drive one day I saw a rental sign for a house at 512 East 88th Street. It was a small apartment with a garden that I took immediately. Eddie, who was still in my life, was happy because we were now spending more time together and he helped me by paying the rent for a year. Later, when he rose within the Kosher Nostra and formed Levy, Adler & Cohen, an insurance company, he bought a luxury high rise apartment at 1725 York Avenue where I also spent periods of time.

I started a relationship with Gino, the thug who had threatened me after the rat attack on Mark and who had continued to come to our old building from time to time as he never stopped working for the real estate manager. I don't really know how or why I became his lover. I knew he was dangerous but there was something about him that attracted me and piqued my curiosity. He was Sicilian and, despite it being said that he was born in Libya, and although he wasn't very tall, he was good-looking with his dark hair and his intense look. It was without doubt a mistake. As well as being 'muscle' for the Mafia, Gino was also a compulsive gambler with serious money problems and he started to turn up at Eddie's high rise apartment and tried to fix some of his horse races.

Things became very bad between Gino and me. One day he even hit me and shot me with the .38 calibre pistol that he always carried. I had to defend myself and pushed him away with my own weapon, putting a bullet through the Gucci jacket he always wore. I thought I had killed him but he survived. On 20 July 1976 he threw me down the stairs, making me lose his unborn child. I filed a report and on 11 August he was arrested but released shortly afterwards. Monica and Mark had been witness to the attack and I realised that this was no life for them so I sent them to Germany for several months to try to distance them from a world that was inappropriate for my children.

The Code of Silence

In those days subpoenas to give evidence in political investigations fell thick and fast and some of the people who really knew some inconvenient things began to turn up dead, taking their secrets to the grave. The fate of Dorothy Kilgallen comes to mind; she was a journalist who had gone to Dallas after the assassination of Kennedy and had gained Jack Ruby's confidence. In 1965, after interviewing Oswald's assassin in prison, she returned to New York and was found dead in her home from an overdose of alcohol and barbiturates. She had no history of alcoholism or barbiturate use. I also remembered the assassination of Sam Giancana on 19 June 1975 at his house in Chicago. The Church Committee wanted to call him to testify but they didn't have time to speak to him. Someone shot him several times, including around the mouth. The message couldn't have been clearer.

The Law of Silence hadn't ceased to apply. On 7 August 1976, a chained barrel full of holes was found in the bay at Dumbfolding, near Miami. When it was opened up, it was found to contain the body of Johnny Rosselli, the same *Mr Hollywood* who had given me the tablets to kill Fidel. He had testified twice before the Church Committee in 1975 about the attempted assassination and his relationship with the Mafia and the CIA. He had testified in April 1976 as well with questions, on that particular occasion, leading towards a supposed conspiracy around the assassination of Kennedy. Senators wanted to return to that subject again but on 28 July he disappeared and his next appearance was as a body in a barrel strangled and shot. Shortly afterwards someone put a copy of an article with news about Rosselli under my door with the message 'You'll be next'. The threats were enough for the New York police to put guards on my house and for Senator Richard Schweiker, who was a member of the Intelligence Committee in the Upper House and whose people had interviewed me after Rosselli's death, to ask for protection for me and my children from the Department of Justice. I always thought that Gino was behind the attacks and had come to my apartment and stolen documents and tapes of telephone conversations that I had recorded to protect myself from him or from Eddie, from lawyers and editors who were beginning to show interest in my story and from investigators sent by Congress, who I began talking to in 1975.

Second Trip to Madrid

In those troubled times I also faced constant pressure from Monica who continually insisted on trying to see her father again and I ended up giving in and organising a trip to Spain. In February 1977 we went back to Madrid, where, unlike the first time, we didn't know where Marcos was. We knew he had bought a house but we didn't know the address. It occurred to me that we could find him through the US Embassy, where I was sure they would follow his every step. But when I asked for details, they voiced their opposition to our trying to contact him and made it clear that they didn't want us to see him, although I explained that if I didn't see him we wouldn't have any money to return home to the United States.

Monica insisted that we shouldn't give up and we went to the Venezuelan Embassy. My daughter was a teenager by now, almost fifteen years old, and used her charms to flirt with the young civil servants. She was the one who secretly got us the address which located Marcos in a mansion in the La Moraleja area. We left happily and decided to go back to the hotel and leave our surprise visit to Marcos until the next day. That was our mistake.

The next morning there was a knock at the door of our room and, when we opened it, we were confronted by two enormous US Marines with automatic rifles who insisted we go with them, without leaving us any room to refuse or negotiate with them. They took the bag, Monica and me and held us by the arm. They put us into a waiting car and drove us to the airport. It didn't make any difference that we protested all the way there, explaining that we hadn't broken any law. They boarded us on a plane that carried no identifying airline logo. They told me never to come back and threw us out of the country. A couple of weeks later, I received an invoice from the US government, from the State Department to be precise, for $3,000 for air transport and a warning that they wouldn't renew my passport if I didn't pay.

Monica was exhausted from crying and said she just wanted to see her father at least once. Her tears and her emptiness never ended. Marcos Pérez Jiménez died in Madrid on 20 September 2001 without his daughter ever having the opportunity to go back and meet him.

Death As a Business

We were back in New York and a few months later I received several calls from Frank Sturgis. After the articles were published, he had started prowling around again and called me frequently and this time he telephoned me to urge me to come back and work for him again. He was on his way to Angola where they were organising forces to fight Fidel and he wanted me to infiltrate and get information. He assured me there was 'good money' in the mission and insisted at least a couple of times, calling me once from Paris in July and again from Lisbon. I refused to go with him because I wanted nothing to do with his battles but also because I had received a call from a man called John Stockwell, head of the CIA station in Angola, who had warned me that Sturgis wasn't in the country at all.

I should have known that my refusal would have consequences and not just for me. In revenge for this, Frank started to sniff around Eddie's businesses and it didn't take him long to find out that Levy, Adler & Cohen, his insurance firm, was plagued with irregularities. It is impossible to believe that it was a coincidence that the authorities began an investigation and legal prosecution around that time which ended with Eddie going to prison, sentenced for fraud and knowing that millions of dollars that had been collected for alleged insurance policies that had really gone to Swiss bank accounts and other places. From the prison where he served his two-year sentence, Eddie sent me a letter 'thanking' me for putting my 'CIA colleagues' on to him. I had no doubt about who it really was because Sturgis said to me once without any feeling of guilt,

'I destroyed your boyfriend because you wouldn't go to Angola.'

That made me think about Rorke and I replied,

'The same way you destroyed Alex?'

He didn't answer that but I have always thought he was behind it. Killing was Sturgis's business. I know for a fact that he killed Rolando Masferrer, *El Tigre,* who died in October 1975 in a car bomb in Miami, and I can state that with a good deal of certainty because on one occasion Frank confessed it to me.

Quite often in our conversations he reminded me that it would be better to keep my mouth shut and he emphasised this in unsubtle ways, saying things like 'you know we're both guilty'. Obviously he was covering his own back. One of the lines of investigation the Rockefeller Commission had pursued had concerned the possibility that Frank and Howard Hunt had been in Dallas together, something that both men denied in their statements under oath, but Gaeton Fonzi, one of the investigators who worked for the senators in the Church Committee, found something that perhaps confirmed his suspicions that Sturgis and Hunt — Fiorini and Eduardo to me — may have committed perjury when he reread the accounts that Meskil had written. I was able to put two and two together not only in the

Everglades but in the city in which Kennedy had been assassinated.

I spoke to Fonzi several times while he was working for the Church Committee and he went on to work for the Special Committee on Political Assassinations in the House of Representatives, which investigated the Kennedy assassinations in 1978. He started coming to the apartment on 88th Street with Al González, another investigator for the Committee, to interview me and examine documents. Frank's calls became more frequent. He told me that Fonzi actually worked for the CIA and he kept insisting that I should say nothing or, if I would not do that, to at least say what he wanted me to say and cover up what he was involved in. Old hands in a world in which no one trusted anyone and where there was little protection, Frank and I both recorded our conversations without telling each other.

A Gunslinger in School Uniform

I thought those tapes would protect me and I didn't pay too much attention to what was going on in my own house. Monica was a teenager and had always felt that Frank was lethal. She said he had 'the eyes of a dead man' and I remember that I often said

265

things like 'when I'm not here any more' . . . She clearly picked up on my fear that something was going to happen to me and she thought Frank was the person threatening to kill me. So she embarked on her own war, after hearing those calls, believing that Sturgis was coming to kill me to stop me talking to Fonzi.

I had taught my children to handle guns, dismantle them, clean them and load them. At that time, Monica went to the Loyola Institute, a Catholic school in Park Avenue which many of the children of gangsters also attended, and, through the brother of a friend, managed to get a .22 calibre gun that took seven bullets. Now armed, she thought 'the right thing to do' was to protect her mother by doing 'whatever was necessary'. I have always sworn that her intention wasn't to kill Sturgis but to 'stop' him. My daughter was very clever. She knew that as a minor the laws that applied to her would be more lenient than if she had been an adult.

On 31 October 1977, Monica positioned herself between some cars in front of my house, waiting for Sturgis to turn up. A neighbour must have seen her from their window with a gun in her hand and called the police, who had also received a call from my lover Frank Smith, who I had telephoned after Monica had called me and told me her plans. My daughter fled and set off a police operation that closed several streets before she was cornered, but she asked to negotiate her surrender with an officer she knew through my work, Terry McSwiggin. To her, he was Uncle Terry and, according to Monica, he was good to her; he took the bullets out of the gun and cleaned the weapon. Thus disarmed, my daughter was handcuffed and taken to the police station. She was still wearing her school uniform.

A few hours later, Sturgis came to my apartment and was arrested, accused of harassment and coercion, in effect of 'instilling fear to prevent a witness testifying before a legally constituted authority', referring to the Special Committee in Congress. He was sent to prison after bail was set at a significant $25,000, which was then reduced to $10,000, and he ended up on the front pages of the newspapers again, although on 4 November a judge dismissed all charges and set him free.

Under Guard and In Fear Again
My life seemed to be sufficiently under threat for the authorities to place me under

guard and give me protection. In the middle of the night, they collected me, my children and Charmaine Burns, a friend from my partying days, a beautiful and sweet woman originally from New Orleans who happened to be staying with us at the time. They flew us to a place in Florida where they had a group of safe houses, Miami Spring Villa, which we weren't allowed to leave at all. It's the life of a prisoner that you are obliged to live when they are under protection, a life of silence when no one tells you anything and the only answer they give you when you ask how long you are going to be cooped up is 'until things calm down'.

With two officers on guard on each shift, you would imagine that there wasn't a lot that could happen to you, although in my case at that time it led to an incident that had nothing to do with the immediate threat to me but also put my life in danger. One Friday night, the officers went to a bar and left us without anyone on watch. A man who was completely mad who had escaped from a mental institution broke into the house. After entering anther apartment and raping and killing the wife of a police officer — something I only found out about afterwards — the man came into our apartment. I was asleep and I woke up to find the man naked and holding a knife to my side, saying dirty things to me, playing with himself and telling me to have sex with him. I was terrified, paralysed, but I realised that he wasn't one of Sturgis's soldiers and I started to talk to him calmly, making him think I was going to give him what he wanted and only asking that we do it in another room. I took a knife, which I always carried with me, from my clothing, opened it and went for him, cutting him superficially three or four times but not deeply enough to make him bleed much. Hysterical with hatred and fear, I called out for Steve Czukas, a customs agent with whom I collaborated as an informant in those days, while I continued to attack the man with the knife. He was forced back out into the street and finally fell to the ground and I managed to close the door. Then he came up to one of the windows and started banging on it, screaming, 'I'm going to kill you! I'll kill you!' He was screaming, I was screaming, my children were screaming, Charmaine was screaming . . . I picked up an emergency telephone that was in the house and asked for help and dozens of agents suddenly appeared in unmarked cars. When they arrived they found me still paralysed with fear and unable to open my hand to let go of the knife, which I only did when I saw Monica and realised that the madman hadn't gone into her room and assaulted her. We were all alive and unharmed but we needed tranquilisers to get over that savage attack.

The Green Exercise Book

The safety they were supposed to guarantee us had failed spectacularly and they moved us to the penthouse in a hotel in Miami, a honeymoon suite where we stayed for a few days. I was mentally exhausted and also worried because my mother was on her own in New York and had to be admitted to hospital after falling mysteriously ill. However, we still didn't know how long we had to stay there until we would be free once again to move around. During that period of uncertainty, Czukas gave me a little green children's exercise book and suggested that I use the time to write, telling me it was the best therapy he could think of, although his apparent disinterest was not quite as it might have seemed. Czukas knew Frank Sturgis well. He had arrested him on several occasions and had told me about a drugs network in Mexico in which he was implicated. He also knew about the trip to Dallas and admitted that he was going to give the exercise book with whatever I had written in it to the Special Committee on Political Assassinations in Washington.

During the next few days I filled sixteen pages with recollections of the trip to Dallas, about my mother, about Fidel, about Marcos Pérez Jiménez and that damned David Walters' betrayal and I realised that it was therapeutic. I started to get back to normal and to feel better. I was offered a new identity, to go into one of those programmes where you can change state and even be given plastic surgery and begin a new life. With an 'I don't have any boyfriends left', I asked if they could send me to Cuba. I felt like joking with them because I knew they would say no. I not only had no interest in going to Arizona but I felt morally obliged to look after mama. I didn't want to leave Frank Smith and our relationship and I had a dysfunctional but in some ways normal life with Eddie.

My First Ending

When I went back to New York, the first thing I did was remove mama from the Lennox Hill Hospital, where she had been admitted, and take her to Eddie's apartment where I converted a bedroom into something comparable to any hospital room. We never knew exactly what had happened to her but I have always suspected that it was some kind of dirty trick which involved Frank Nelson and, of course, Sturgis. While I was in protective custody, mama had complained of some discomfort which she thought was a result of sitting in front of the air conditioning and the two Franks took her to a doctor in Park Avenue where, she told me, they gave her an injection. After that, she started to show signs of paralysis and her whole body was becoming weak, although her mind was functioning perfectly well. Her usual doctor agreed with me in thinking someone had given her something that had affected her nervous system and Monica also thought that the unnecessary injection had contained some kind of poison. Anyway, she began to fade rapidly and, as I didn't want to take her to a hospital, I employed a nurse to help me because mama was bedridden and I wanted to care for her as best as I could. Whenever possible I carried her to a wheelchair to walk along the East River, combed her hair to make her look beautiful and managed to make her laugh from time to time.

She died in my arms on 7 December 1977 and it wasn't just the end for her but it was also the end for me. In a way, I died with her. She had been my pillar, my rock, the only person I had been able to talk to truthfully about my life although there were many times when we argued, when I caused her great unhappiness with the decisions I made and the excessive weight of responsibility they placed on her.

I discovered that she kept secrets that would prove to be very painful as well. When I began to go through the beautiful trunks from the 1920s that she had filled with mementos, in the lining of one of them I found an envelope with the word *Peaches* written on it, the affectionate nickname she gave me. When I opened it I started to cry inconsolably. There was a photograph of a three-year-old child who looked exactly like Fidel. I knew straight away that she had known her whole life that my first child had survived.

My first reaction was wild anger, an explosion of fury. How could she have kept that information from me? How could she have left me in such agonising doubt? She had no right! When I calmed down a little, I read a note that she had written, clearly not long ago, in which she referred to Monica and Mark, who had only been born eight years before. Mama told me to focus on looking after my two children and not to worry about this one. She assured me that he was all right. Reading and rereading her words, I looked at that photograph, thinking about little Monica and Beegie, and I calmed down and began to understand what she was saying. I think she was trying to protect me so that I didn't go mad. She probably did what I would have done myself. I understood her motives in some way and I forgave her. I loved her like no one else.

I was certain of one thing: I couldn't live without her. I was sad, broken, destroyed, and from then on I felt absolutely miserable. Monica, who had spent so much of her teens with mama, identifies that day as the moment our lives changed, when we fell off a cliff into a spiral of misery. We had as normal a life as we could and even adjusted to another period of extreme poverty and then one anxiety began to follow another — evictions, a nomadic life and desperation when we didn't even have anything to eat.

An Impossible Escape
The death of mama shook my life up like an earthquake and left me without a foundation, something I needed more than ever at that time. The pressure of the investigations into the assassination of Kennedy was intensifying and various forces were pulling me in different directions. I didn't want to

cross paths with Sturgis and all the Cubans again but I was afraid of incriminating myself and being accused of a crime because of issues like the armoury robberies, and the only thing I could think of doing was to escape.

So I took my children and went to the Bahamas, believing that no summons would reach me there. The sea wasn't a big enough barrier and they came looking for me. My brother Joe insisted I come back and reminded me that I could end up in prison if I kept ignoring the summons. At that time he had a very close relationship with Howard Baker, the Republican senator for Tennessee who in 1973 had posed the key question in the Watergate investigation, 'what did the President know and when did he know it?', which would end up toppling Nixon. Between the two of them, they convinced me that running away from a federal summons would make me look guilty and would mean I'd have to run for the rest of my life and that, one way or another, I couldn't avoid being pursued for ever and would end up in prison. Baker got me a lawyer and I went back, willing to testify, although, Lawrence Krieger, the lawyer in charge of all matters relating to Teddy Kennedy's property matters, didn't like me at all, it was he who managed to get the Committee to give me something that would allow me to speak without fear of incriminating myself: an immunity order, number 78/0136, which was issued on 1 May 1978.

At the end of that month I boarded a plane to Washington with the children and two small dogs that had just become part of the family. As soon as we landed, an agent was waiting to escort us to a taxi. When the taxi driver asked where we were going, Mark said the first hotel name that came to mind and so we ended up at the Regency.

The Special Committee on Assassinations in the House of Representatives

Why was I obliged to return and testify before Congress after so many years? In 1976, it was believed that the investigation committee was, to some extent, a cross between the Church Committee and the Hart-Schweiker Committee, both of which were focused on investigating the assassinations of the President. Since the Warren Committee had concluded in 1964 that Lee Harvey Oswald was not part of any conspiracy, many indignant voices had been raised demanding to know the truth.

The body known as the HSCA was created in response to civil pressure and the hundreds of articles, documents and books that had appeared since 1963 speculating about a conspiracy originating deep within the government to kill Kennedy and another one to do the same to Martin Luther King. The investigations by the Committee lasted from 1978 to 1979 and a report was made public afterwards.

On 31 May 1978 we arrived at the Capitol where my children sat on benches in the room, each one holding their pet, and the interrogation, in which thirty-six delegates participated, began. They had the green exercise book that Czukas suggested I write in, although they had deleted some of its contents, especially the names of CIA agents, allegedly to protect national security. To the irritation of the members of the Committee, Fonzi had also made his own deletions and notes. There was a slide projector in the room on which we were shown photographs in which I could identify Ozzie, as I had known Lee Harvey Oswald, for instance, in the Everglades. They were thorough and they questioned every area: Fidel, the thefts from the armouries, the trip to Dallas . . . Some of them were very hard on me and questioned me relentlessly, throwing doubt on my statements and trying to confuse me. But I felt comforted when one of those who had been particularly aggressive, Christopher Dodd, apologised when he met me in the corridor during one of the breaks:

'I'm sorry,' he said, 'I know you're telling the truth.'

Dodd was in fact one of the Committee members who published a note expressing his disagreement when a report was presented, concluding that 'Lee Harvey Oswald fired three shots at President John F. Kennedy', that 'the second and third shots hit the President' and 'the third shot killed the President'. Dodd explained that he voted against it because the ballistics report on the rifle that Ozzie allegedly used, a Mannlicher–Carcano, showed that it was impossible to fire consecutive shots with this model weapon.

In addition, based on the testimony of more than twenty witnesses and an audio tape, the HSCA concluded that there had been a fourth shot and, therefore, a second shooter and that Kennedy had probably died as a result of a conspiracy, although it stated that it was 'unable to identify the other shooters or the extent of the conspiracy'. They ruled out emphatically, reverting to the new evidence available to them, that either the Russian or Cuban governments had anything to do with it. They also concluded that the exiled anti-Castro Cubans and organised crime were not involved either, although the Committee didn't rule out 'the possibility' that there may have been 'individuals' involved who were linked to organisations in exile or the Mafia.

I just did what I thought I had to do. A few days after appearing and testifying, I sent a correction about a date in which I had allegedly seen Oswald because I had made an error under pressure and they wanted to create doubts about my credibility. Finishing it was a relief.

I can also laugh when I remember some of the details such as one that my daughter, Monica, likes to mention. I wanted to look elegant and presentable when I testified and had spoken to a neighbour in New York, a very polite black man, whom we affectionately called 'fine shit' because his apartment was like a shop window for all kinds of stolen property. Among them were delicate fabrics imported from Asia and he decided to have one of them made into a tailored suit for me. I went to the Capitol dressed like a lady in a dark suit of dubious origin.

CHAPTER 9
CHILDREN OF CUBA

After testifying in Congress and returning to New York, I worked for the police for a while. My life sailed at the edge of disaster once again. Monica, who during my wayward years had been looked after by her grandmother, who always tried to give her the serenity my hectic lifestyle and my friends couldn't guarantee, had entered a rebellious period and our relationship became tense. One day she turned up drunk at the apartment on 88th Street and I was very angry with her. I think I even hit her and she ran off. I spent several days not knowing where she was and I thought I was going mad. I even contacted Gino again to ask him to look for her.

She returned on her own accord five days later but I worried about what she had been through. She told me of the people she had been staying with and their involvement in prostitution. Though she managed to get out of there without ever becoming involved, it was a traumatic experience for the both of us.

Financially, it was a very difficult time and the sun shone on me when Thomas Guinzburg, one of the co-founders of *The Paris Review* who was then running Viking Press, put an offer on the table to do a book on my story. Gaeton Fonzi, the investigator who worked for Congress, was also interested in writing one but I didn't want him to do it. I think it was good decision because years later, when he wrote his account of the facts relating to the Kennedy assassination, *The Last Investigation,* I didn't come out of it very well. The contract that Guinzburg offered me was very generous as well, $340,000, so I accepted it. I received an advance of $75,000 and with this I bought a car and put down a deposit for a house in Darien, Connecticut, a pretty property at 86 Maywood Road. I moved in with Monica and Mark and I was able to keep a garden and satisfy my love of animals by keeping pigs, goats, ducks and horses.

It was a peaceful life; I would even say it was a dream life. But I had too much of a past to go back to being an ordinary housewife. My Mafiosi friends, for example, used the property from time to time to hide trucks when they were affected by the second oil crisis of that period and were illegally transporting fuel. In spite of my having moved, the harassment didn't stop and not only because I had gone to Congress to answer all the questions they put to me and openly provide names of people who would have preferred to remain in the shadows, but because, to top it all, I was about to write a book. One day, when Monica was doing her homework in the kitchen wearing one of my jackets, a shot was fired through the window that almost killed her. We never knew who was responsible and all we heard was someone escaping on a motorcycle. On another occasion, most of my animals died suddenly. The only thing I am sure about was that it wasn't the Mafia.

The harassment was constant and I had serious problems keeping up the mortgage payments because although I started writing the book several times, I couldn't deliver it and the publisher lost interest. The only thing they wanted from the book was to revive the idea that Kennedy's assassination wasn't what the public had been told and they wanted to use a photograph on the cover that Alex Rorke had taken in the Everglades in which you could see Sturgis, Hemming and me with Ozzie and others.

The problem was that I had only one good copy of that photo but I had given it to Senator Baker. The other copy was of poorer quality and, on top of all that, Gino had stolen it when he took documents and tapes from my house.

All this led me to take the decision to leave the house and return to New York where I had kept the apartment on 88th Street. I had only one pony and a goat that had survived the slaughter so I decided to take them with me to the city. Keeping a goat at home was odd enough but I could manage it. It was impossible to keep the pony so I thought I would give it away. I asked Frank Smith, my policeman lover, to get me one of those trailers for transporting horses and I took the animal from Connecticut to New York where I was going to leave it at the zoo. Although we arrived at the Central Park Zoo past their closing time, the staff there took in the pony and goat and kept them together in the 'Children's Zoo' portion of the park for as long as they could. Later they were transferred to Flushing Meadow's Park in Queens where one terrible winter the goat and pony froze to death, huddled together, as the heater for their stall had failed.

Return to Fidel

The serious financial problems I now had were leaving me with few options and one of those that I had was to try to turn to Fidel, ask him for help and to go back to Cuba. I went to the Cuban legation in front of the United Nations several times to take letters that I wanted to have delivered to him. Somehow, I never lost hope. When I left the mission building after one of my visits, I was stopped by a short man with red hair. His name was Larry Wack, an ambitious FBI agent who was a leading member of the anti-terrorist squad and wanted me to stop visiting the legation. He also wanted me to work for him and to infiltrate Omega 7, the anti-Castro terrorist group that had been founded in New Jersey by Eduardo Arocena and which had committed several attacks. I saw Wack several times and I never liked him. I thought he drank too much and he acted dishonourably on a number of occasions, which I will never forgive him for.

In that period of 1979, a rumour began to circulate that Fidel was going to come back to New York, this time to give a lecture at the United Nations, and I knew it was true when two secret service agents called at my door and told me that I was ordered to leave the city. With Castro visiting, they wanted to reduce the potential for problems and they gave me three hours to leave. I told them it was impossible because I had no money so they gave me some. It wasn't much. Despite that, I took the children and the dogs, put our things in some boxes and left for Canada. Fidel's silence in response to my letters left me with no illusions and I had to think of my children. I had thought about leaving everything behind so many times and this seemed like a good opportunity. The government was going to pay for my 'trip to freedom', although it was also going to waste money sending a couple of cars with four agents to follow me on my journey to Montreal. During the journey, I made the decision to try to contract Fidel again.

The journey to Canada was long and tiring and as soon as we crossed the border we stopped to rest at a small French hotel. Then, even though the Agency tail remained behind our car, we went to 1415 Pine Street where there was a Cuban legation. I went in with the children and handed over our passports. I said that my life was being threatened and explained that I was a friend of Fidel and wanted to go back to Cuba with my children. I even signed a document which stipulated that if anything happened to me I would leave my children in Fidel's custody and asked that they were sent to Cuba.

At the legation they started to make arrangements but they told me that I had to finalise the applications and get visas in Washington. I had to get everything to the Office of Cuban Interests which was in the Czechoslovakian Embassy on 16th Street in the capital and that's what I did, although I had to wait in Canada for two or three days until Fidel, who was giving his lecture on 12 October at the UN, left New York. On the way back to the United States, when I crossed the border I was interrogated but they let me go and I reached the Czech Embassy in Washington. I had brought a bag full of documents that showed my relationship with Fidel, from photos and love letters to other mementos and I left them there when I got the visas. I still regret being separated from those treasured possessions.

When I left the embassy, Wack was waiting for me with some other FBI agents. He threatened to arrest me for conspiracy if I contacted the Cubans again although I defended myself, saying that he had no legal basis for detaining me and that I had family in Cuba. I even dared to tell him, ironically, that we were going to the island for Monica's educational project which was to investigate 'a green snake that was lethally poisonous' (a reference to Fidel and his green military uniform). He didn't laugh, not even a little bit.

Wack and the others weren't my only problem. The biggest challenge was that I didn't have the money to get to the island although I now had the documents to allow me to go there. I had no option to return to New York because our house in Connecticut had been ransacked. Not long after our return to Manhattan, the garden apartment next to ours, 510 East 88th Street, was firebombed. Obviously, whoever meant us harm had gotten the wrong address. As we had nowhere else to go we stayed at 512 and things became increasingly difficult for me and my family. With no money at all, they had cut off the electricity and we were left with nothing. I had to go to Social Services and ask for assistance in order to eat. Our poverty was such that we had to beg and steal to feed ourselves. It was a very difficult time, possibly the hardest of my life, days of full of anxiety and misery when we were without power for six weeks.

Nor did the harassment stop. 'Friends' of

Tommy *Tea Balls* Mancusco and Tony *Ducks* Corallo sometimes gave me money and food and let themselves be seen in public with me to send the message that they were on my side and supported me but, even so, the attacks continued. A tall, blond man who called himself Sam used to prowl around the building and had been asking questions about me before the fire. I always suspected that he was working for the CIA. I felt that they were still insisting that I keep my mouth shut and, to get me out of the way, they wanted to take me to the limit and push me to commit suicide. They didn't succeed, although I was on the verge of desperation many times.

One day in 1980, I was called to One Police Plaza, the central headquarters of the police in New York. They put a sheet of blank paper in front of me and insisted that I sign it. I was so desperate that I did it and then they said to me:

'Now you'll have the opportunity to see what your boyfriend is doing.'

The *Marielitos*
What I had just signed was a document that they would fill in afterwards and as a result of which I would start to collaborate with the armed forces of the United States

which, at that time, was starting to prepare military bases to face the phenomenon known as the *marielitos'*. On 1 April, a group of five Cuban citizens managed to get political asylum in the Peruvian Embassy in Havana following an assault on the building. Fidel demanded that they be returned and, when this was refused, he removed the legation's diplomatic immunity three days later. Immediately, hundreds of Cubans sought refuge in the embassy and that soon became thousands. Fidel then gave free passage so that any Cuban who wanted to leave could do so, as long as they had someone who would sponsor them and take charge of them. Mariel Port became a launching point from which thousands of Cubans left for Key West in Florida and landed in the United States.

I moved in with my sister Valerie, who was living in Harrisburg in Pennsylvania, and she introduced me to Major Wayne Bradshaw who she had met when he was working with Vietnamese refugees in a job similar to the one he was to carry out with the Cubans.

After a single interview, he made me a 'marshal' and I started working in a base, Fort Indiantown Gap, one of the enclaves in which the US authorities started to gather the *marielitos* while they processed each case and found a use for them. They gave me a uniform, boots and military training and I had to get their passports, take their fingerprints and make identity cards. In many cases I had to use my knowledge of Spanish to try to find out about their personal history and note down the number that many had tattooed on the insides of their lips, the indelible reminder of their stay in prison in Cuba. It was known that Fidel had sent criminals in the exodus and not just to get rid of them. He intended to send a message to whoever abandoned the revolution or betrayed him that they were the dregs of society. And it was also a way of punishing his enemy in the north.

I lived between my sister's house and the base, which looked fuller by the day. The American authorities were overwhelmed and completely unprepared and didn't know what to do with all the Cubans continually arriving, 125,000 between April and September, and for whom there wasn't enough room. The facilities were clearly inadequate for separating the population into different groups: children, women, families, homosexuals . . . To make the situation worse, there were serious medical problems. Not only were there mentally ill people among the refugees who had been treated with antipsychotic drugs but others who had become addicted to the antidepressants they had been being given to combat the severe depression of which many of them were showing signs.

Worse Than Cuba

I spent less than a year there, after which they transferred me to Fort Chaffee, Arkansas, the only base that was situated in a place where the climate was generally hot and where they sent many of the mentally ill, retarded, physically disabled, homosexual or elderly Cubans. I got an apartment because I wouldn't let Mark live at the base as he was still a minor and I started work. What I saw on some days revived ghosts from my past, broke my heart and made me suffer enormously. I was in charge of 600 children who were lodged in two enormous barracks and I learned with horror that they didn't know how to treat them. The little ones cried a lot, unable to come to terms with being separated from their parents. The military's response to tears, an anguish I knew only too well because I had shed them and felt the same way in Drangstedt, was to inject the children with something that rendered them unconscious for a couple of days. After their stay at the base, they sent them to orphanages all over the United States or handed them over to someone who was happy to sponsor them and then they let them go, giving them $3,000 and Social Security cards and health care but also a considerable baggage of hatred and confusion.

In Fort Chaffee I saw scenes of real terror that will never be erased from my memory, such as the death of a child from a simple asthma attack or the image of a pregnant woman who was kept in handcuffs. I also realised that those who were in charge didn't understand the magnitude of the problem, the challenges and the personal dramas that they should have dealt with more humanely.

I couldn't remain silent. I argued frequently with the military officers. I got involved in problems every time I opened my mouth to report abuses or mistakes and I was subjected to a military judicial process because once I transported a severely wounded boy who had been attacked with a machete to a hospital outside of the base, and in doing so I revealed to the locals that there were Cuban refugees being kept at the base.

Conditions were atrocious and I couldn't

avoid thinking of Bergen-Belsen, although the food given to the Cubans was better than in Hitler's camps and they didn't carry out the same atrocities. It was impossible not to recall it. There was a similar air of misery, confinement, overcrowding and desperation. For many, it was a tragic and unbearable situation and there were also many suicides which deepened the tremendous sense of sadness. I saw adult men crying inconsolably and continually writing letters of their desire to return to their own country, admitting that they regarded the journey to the United States as a mistake and declaring 'it's worse than Cuba'.

Among the population in the base were many Cubans who were absolute geniuses, brilliant and intelligent people who spoke two or three languages. There they could only demonstrate that they were masters of survival in a place where all they were offered was a bunk and a sheet. There was no lack of troublesome people, invariably those with tattoos on their lower lips. However, the biggest problem for the federal guards was Santería.

Hated by the Ku Klux Klan
The worst incident at Fort Chaffee occurred when I was sent to the base for the

82nd Airborne Division, among whose ranks were members who represented the worst of the Ku Klux Klan. They could do wonders with a nightstick and the first thing they put into practice was the custom of waking the Cubans up in the middle of the night and carrying out searches, as they did in prison. Supposedly, they were looking for weapons but in reality they were unnecessary and cruel raids in which they destroyed the items associated with their religion of Santería and everything else the Cubans had been able to make. As hard as I tried to stop them, I never managed to get them to listen to me although I did succeed in stopping the abuse of pregnant women. For that, they insulted me frequently, calling me 'a commie-loving liberal'.

Just as had happened to me in my childhood in Washington during the racial disturbances, where they had verbally abused me as well, sometimes denigrating me as a 'nigger lover', they didn't hide their hatred because that would only help the Cubans. It seems unthinkable that it was 1981 but this was the reality at the base and in Barling, the city in which it was located, a place dominated by the Ku Klux Klan and where it wasn't unusual to see T-shirts bearing the slogan 'I Hate Niggers' or 'Hate Niggers'.

On some nights, when it was my turn to be on duty with black soldiers, we could see burning, flaming crosses in the distance.

Mark can testify to the terrifying power that the Klan exercised in Barling. The first day he went to school he not only joined the Hispanic and black children and realised they were being terrorised, but he was given a leaflet by a white child advertising a KKK summer camp that was offering paramilitary training. He didn't go back to the school but he definitely had the opportunity to experience the hatred that ran through the veins of those people when, one day, we went out with one of the federal guards at the base who turned out to be the 'grand imperial wizard' of the KKK, a leader within the organisation. We were going to shooting practice and the man put a watermelon at a distance as the target and as Mark was about to pull the trigger he leaned in to his ear and said:

'I want you to shoot that piece of fruit like it was the head of a nigger.'

Return to Florida

When my mission at Fort Chaffee came to an end I decided to go back east. Major Bradshaw had come to see me again in Arkansas, saying that, when his work had finished there, he would be going back and starting work with the department in the National Security Agency, the NSA, specializing in Cuba. I didn't particularly want to be a part of that venture but as I had nowhere to live I took Mark and went back to Valerie who had then moved from Pennsylvania to Virginia after marrying a former soldier. Their marriage quickly ran into difficulties and, after a few short months, the marriage was over.

Valerie decided to relocate to Florida and, after a brief time living in New York, Mark and I joined here there. I had to drive a car that I had got through Bradshaw, a government vehicle with which, after saying I didn't want to work for the NSA, I had accumulated thousands of dollars' worth of debt through mileage and the use of gasoline cards. Without knowing how I was going to get out of that, I took the car south and drove it into a lake in Winter Haven, the place where we were going to settle in Florida. Obviously that wasn't a good idea. One day, Mike Minto, a special agent in Florida, appeared at the door. He informed me that the accumulated debt amounted to some $12,000 and that I could be accused of fraud. When I explained that I had no money to pay it, he told me that I would have to work for them so I started to work with the DEA, the US drug enforcement agency fighting the war against drug trafficking.

'Fidel, It's Me'

While I was in Florida I couldn't get my experiences with the *marielitos* out of my head. They had made me realise that it didn't matter how much time passed: I would never be able to get Cuba out of me. I carried it inside me and it was always close by. The desire to go to the island was growing inside me. It was decided that I should go back, twenty-two years after my first meeting one afternoon in February 1959 with that tall, bearded man with the intense stare and an irresistible smile. My intention was that Monica, who was now almost twenty, would go with me but her visa application was refused, possibly because of her surname, Pérez Jiménez, and it weighed very heavily on me to leave her behind to go to Fidel's country. However, I had an open visa that the Office of Cuban Interests in the Czech Embassy had approved in 1979.

In September 1981, deliberately wearing a red shirt and a black jacket in the colours of the flag of the 26th of July Movement, I boarded a plane in Miami. I felt like the relatives of Cubans who, in those days, after going through a slow and lengthy bureaucratic process in which every last detail was scrutinised, were able to fly happily because President Jimmy Carter had lifted travel restrictions in 1977 that Ronald Reagan imposed again in 1982. Like them, I was also filled with happiness although the flight made me tense and a little nervous because I didn't really know what I was doing.

As soon as we landed in Havana, some agents tapped me on the shoulder and asked me to go with them. They took me to a small room along a corridor past a sign saying that it was the diplomatic channel. There were two guards, including a soldier armed with an AK-47 rifle. I was met only with silence when I asked questions or demanded to see Fidel and I was sweating profusely, wrapped again in the tropical heat and humidity. Even so, I was not worried. At the point I was absolutely calm and felt a complete absence of fear. Guards kept arriving but I sensed that they were going to take me to see Castro. If there had been any threat at all or something that I should have been frightened of, there was no sign of it. When one of the guards gave me a glass of water, he took a few sips himself to show that it wasn't poisoned. I wasn't even worried about that.

Without a word, we left that room and José Martí Airport where they hadn't even opened my suitcase to see what I had brought with me. We got into a car that smelled of new leather and, accompanied by four agents, I travelled to an unknown destination. I didn't bother to ask where we were going because I knew I wouldn't get an answer. After twenty-five minutes we came to an elegant house with columns, a satellite dish, two guards at the back and a metal wire gate. I walked in behind the soldiers who had brought me there and an elderly couple, whom I didn't at first recognise, greeted me. When I looked at them more closely I realised it was Mr and Mrs Fernández, Fidel's English teachers with whom I had spent some time in 1959. We gave each other a very heartfelt embrace. They were very old now and lived simply, but they were sweet to me and offered a small serving of rice and beans, water and a tough piece of meat. That dish brought home to me the economic poverty of the island.

They took me up to a room and when I tried to open my suitcase one of the soldiers made a gesture to indicate that I shouldn't do it. I could smell Fidel's cigars and I started to feel anxious and ask about him but they just said to me, 'wait, wait'. Then I heard footsteps and voices talking rapidly in Spanish and my nerves started to overwhelm me. Then the door opened and I saw a man with grey hair. It was him, Fidel. I got upset and started to cry, overcome with emotion and not knowing what was going to happen.

He stepped up to me and said with a pointed brevity:

'Hello, stop crying.'

Fidel had never been able to stand it when I cried. I could only think of one thing to say to him in response:

'Fidel, it's me.'

He shook hands with me, walked about the room, turned round and looked at me intently, which made me feel very uncomfortable because I didn't know what he was thinking. Then he sat down on a chair and said:

'You came back.'

I went up to him, knelt down and put my head in his lap. I could tell he wasn't very happy to see me, was possibly even a bit annoyed, but for me it was like a miracle. I started talking with tears in my eyes.

'I need to find answers, Fidel. I want to

know about our son. I need to know if he ever existed, if he's alive or dead. I can't live my whole life not knowing because it's like a hole in my soul. If he's alive, I would like to know him. I have to see him. I'll tear up my passport if necessary . . .'

I showed him photos of Mark and Monica. I opened the suitcase to take out the presents I had bought for our son. I kept talking between sobs . . . Fidel seemed unmoved and all he said to me was:

'He's fine. All children here belong to Cuba.'

His serious manner didn't hurt me then. On the contrary, it was enough, the closest I had ever got to a response to the biggest and most frustrating question of my life, the first ray of light in the darkest of chapters.

Andrés, at Last

Fidel signalled to one of the guards who acknowledged him and they spoke to each other. He told me that he had to go and, when he got up, he opened the door to a tall youngster. He was a little slimmer than my son Mark, with black, slightly curly hair, wearing a blue shirt, khaki trousers, Chinese slippers and carrying a couple of books under his arm. Fidel then said:

'Andrés.'

We shook hands. I wasn't absolutely sure what I was looking at but I couldn't stop staring at the young man who said something like, 'welcome to Cuba'. With no time for pleasantries after so many years of uncertainty, I asked him a little doubtfully:

'Am I your mother?'

He looked at me and embraced me and I broke down into a flood of uncontrollable tears while he tried to calm me down.

'Don't cry any more,' he said, but his words just made me sob even more.

I couldn't stop looking at the young man, at his hands, his face, that nose that was exactly like Fidel's . . . Without any doubt he was his son; he was like a young Fidel. He was our son, I believe that with all certainty, and his image has been forever stamped on my memory since that day.

Fidel walked in and out of the room and let me spend some time with Andrés who told me he was a medical student. I showed him the photos of his brother and sister. I tried to give him the presents I had brought in the suitcase, my shoes and trousers, anything that could be left as a memento. I also told him that I needed to write to him and he gave me an address where I did write to him afterwards and from which a letter came for me, but when I opened the enve-

302

lope it was empty.

Fidel walked down the stairs and I heard him talking with someone below. I never saw him in person again.

When Andrés left, I was alone and couldn't sleep, although I could swear that it was the most exhausting day of my life.

In the morning I went downstairs for breakfast and it was made clear to me that it was best if I left, but first they wanted to know about my experience at Fort Chaffee. Three of Fidel's investigation took me to a private room and I began to answer questions and tell them everything I had seen at the base, writing it down in English; a story of segregation and the mistreatment and abuse of the *marielitos* which left them shocked. I backed up everything with documents that I had taken to confirm what I was telling them.

After that they took me to the airport. I left Cuba and landed in Miami still in shock. Valerie came to pick me up at the airport and she still remembers finding me in a state of agitation, almost hysterical, incapable of doing anything other than repeating over and over again:

'I've seen him, I've seen him. I met Andrés. My son is alive.'

CHAPTER 10
A STORY LIKE A MOVIE

Andrés, the son I had with Fidel, was alive. I had seen him, I had met him. I could finally lay to rest all my doubts together with all the lies and manipulation that I had been subjected to, and although I had had to be separated from him and to sign a document promising to give up any attempt to take him to the United States with me, I was able not only to defend my honesty but also myself as a woman and a mother.

Four FBI agents came to Valerie's house on Eagle Lake and they interviewed me for hours. I described Fidel, Andrés, the house, the room, the guards, with all the numerous details that I could . . . The story I told filled eighteen pages and when we were finished they said:

'We know you're telling the truth because we were there.'

The house where I had seen Fidel and Andrés was under continual surveillance by the CIA. Unfortunately, as with so many other times in my life, the truth I told made things uncomfortable for someone else.

I went to New York to see Monica and to try to convince her to go to Florida with me but, above all, to tell her about her brother and about Cuba as well, a story every bit as emotional and intense as the one I had lived and which I told her while we had a cappuccino in a café. When I got up from the table, I fainted after two or three steps. Monica took me in her arms and started to scream hysterically. She saved my life, finding a taxi and getting me to a hospital quickly. I woke up on a hospital trolley with a drip in my arm and mumbling about my son in Cuba. They wanted to put me under psychiatric supervision for thirty days.

I had had a cardiac arrest and I was always convinced it hadn't been a natural occurrence but, rather, a *present* that the US government gave me to pay me back for having gone back to Cuba. I think my coffee was poisoned with something like scopolamine and it left me with a cardiac arrhythmia as a memento. As on so many other occasions, I have no way of proving it but it looks more than suspicious when someone pays all the hospital bills and all the hospital records of my stay disappear.

The King of Eloise

As soon as I could I returned to Florida alone. Monica didn't want to come and I had sent Mark to live with a friend in Indiana for a while. At that time I smoked and one day I needed some cigarettes and I went to a shop, driving a beat-up car that I had bought for a couple of hundred dollars and that had bullet holes in one side. While driving, I was completely absorbed by a poster advertising Coppertone, the sun protection cream, and I hit a Cadillac, out of which stepped a man of some one hundred kilos plus.

'Young lady, you're going to have to come with me. I'm the sheriff,' he said, looking very serious.

'Can't we just forget it?' I asked, innocently.

'We can call an end to it here nicely if you have dinner with me,' he fired back, cheekily.

I could see perfectly well what kind of man I was dealing with so I agreed and he took me to dinner at an Italian restaurant, but not before taking me to a shop and buying me four cartons of Parliament cigarettes. That's how I came to know Alton Kirkland who was, by his own definition, 'a true marvel for any woman: a delicious and

306

nutritious redneck for all your needs'. He was a clown, a joker and as funny as hell, crude and uncouth, and I didn't stop laughing with him, although he could be a bit cruel, saying things like 'I don't want any lizards here', a reference to blacks, Puerto Ricans, Mexicans and other people who picked oranges and okra on their plantations or looked after their cows. He was a real brute when he spoke but I found it impossible not to give way to his charms and I found it charming when he did things like call himself 'the King of Eloise' or told me he was going to show me the city and when I got there all I saw was an enormous trailer on the side of which he had built a porch.

'I don't need anything else,' he said when I asked him jokingly where the kingdom was that he had told me about. 'What I need is a wife,' he added.

It looked like he already had one, or at least that's what I thought when, on going into the trailer, I met a tattooed woman who went up the wall when she saw me, an outburst that didn't fluster Kirkland one bit.

'What are you doing here? Get out of my house. We're finished. This is my new wife,' he said, by way of introduction.

I realised that the best thing for me to do at that moment was to leave them to sort things out and I went back to Valerie's house, told her that I had just met a madman and admitted that I had fallen for him.

'I didn't know they still made them like that.'

When she heard his name, my sister told me that he owned a large trucking company, Kirkland Transfer, and when he started coming to the house asking for his 'new wife', she suggested that I should stop saying no and accept his offer as I might end up inheriting a truck company. But I didn't want to get married, although I laughed a lot with him and I liked our relationship. I preferred living how I wanted, between the trailer and Valerie's house, which was also shared with her friend Dot, an eccentric woman who always carried a portable television around with her and was addicted to soap operas.

Everything changed when, one day, Gino appeared at my sister's house. He was moving in with her; this was too much for me so I decided to leave and, at that moment, I went to see Kirkland and asked him:

'Where do you want to get married?'

In January 1983, in a discreet civil ceremony in a building in Polk County, I became Ilona M. Kirkland.

Cocaine and Weapons

Gino and my husband soon became good friends. At the time I knew that Kirkland, who was also a bail bondsman, was involved in illegal schemes and businesses. But Gino was Mafia and organised crime exercised an irresistible attraction over my new husband. Before long, he was taking cocaine and transporting marijuana in his trucks and soon he was being scrutinised by the DEA.

After less than three months of marriage, they knocked at the door and when I opened it I saw Minto, the Special Agent from the FDLE, Florida Department of Law Enforcement whom I had met through the incident with the CIA car, and two other agents, including a short man of Italian origin who I believe worked for the Agency. They insisted I accompany them to talk about two unsolved murders. It was a case where they had found the bodies of two people from New York and someone had pointed me out as a suspect. It didn't take long to find out that it was Gino who had given them my name and had also shown them one of the press articles from the 1970's that had a photograph of me with a weapon captioned *'Her orders from CIA: kill Castro'*. They arrested me as a suspect, took my gun and sent it to Tallahassee for analysis. Minto also tried to accuse Mark of murder because my son's fingerprints had been found on the sacks and tape that had been wrapped round the bodies.

We were innocent and we could only wait until they worked it out and proved it. For my part, I knew exactly what had happened. I was sure that Gino had killed the two men because in those days in Florida he was still carrying out contracts for the Mafia in New York. Regarding the suspicion about Mark, he and I could remember perfectly well the day that Gino, who sometimes stayed in our trailer and borrowed our car, had asked my son to give him some plastic bags and sticky tape. We also remembered how, when he arrived with the car smelling of decay, he came up with a story about a dead deer and told Mark to clean the vehicle.

When our innocence was proved, they put us under protective custody because Gino's whereabouts were unknown. He wasn't arrested until December 1983 when he was caught in an undercover operation in which Kirkland and two other people were also arrested. The authorities spent three months investigating my husband because it was

310

discovered that he used his position as a bail guarantor to traffic arms and two officers posing as drug traffickers bought seven guns from him. They were also pursuing the transportation of marijuana in his trucks and when the undercover officers started to talk about drugs and invented a story about someone owing them half a million dollars, Kirkland told them that he had a friend with links to the Mafia who could help them. So that's how the officers met Gino who told them that he was connected to 'the Family' and 'just like in a scene from the end of *The Godfather*', as one of the officers said afterwards, he offered to kill the debtor for $20,000.

As if that wasn't enough to incriminate them, Kirkland agreed to transport and warehouse marijuana for the undercover police officers and Gino tried to sell them five kilos of cocaine. Gino was sentenced to a year in prison while Kirkland, whose lawyer accused me of having set a trap, got five years, although not for the drugs or arms but for buying stolen goods.

Diamonds in Cans

Mark and I were under protection again, working with the authorities in Florida. We spent some time in Tampa where we were taken to live in a complex of apartments whose owners, it turned out, were drug traffickers who moved cocaine around in waterbeds so we ended up once again in a house full of bugs and working for the DEA.

I didn't want to stay there a day longer than necessary. I dug out my address book, picked up the telephone and called Frank Smith, my ex-lover in the police. I had to endure a telling-off and recriminations about how I ended up marrying someone like Kirkland, but Frank said I should go back and he offered to help me. I set off on my way back and I made a stopover in Washington where I contacted Andrew St George, a reporter who had covered Cuba for *Life* magazine and had been in the Sierra Maestra with Fidel and covered the anti-Castro operations there. Che always suspected, as did many others, that he was a CIA agent. He loaned me $5,000 and with that money we moved to Queens to an apartment at 8811 34th Avenue in Jackson Heights.

It was 1984 and Mark was able to go back to school. I met my old boyfriend, Frank Smith, again and began working for Wackenhut, a private investigation agency that I believe was really a cover for FBI operations. The company had its headquarters in

Long Island and I worked for them for a year carrying out different jobs. The first was in a shop selling diamonds where they suspected that someone was stealing from them. I discovered that it was a couple of women who had been employed there for more than fifteen years and they worked in a secured room where they classified the precious stones. Their method was simple: occasionally they dropped some of the diamonds in their cans of drink which they took away with them as if to recycle them; but they didn't take those cans home with them, rattling quietly, for a few pennies or because they were concerned about the environment; they took them for millions of dollars. I had befriended the women and understood their struggle, working for little more than the minimum wage. But I had to pluck up the courage to report them and that was the end of that mission. After that, Wackenhut sent me to undertake surveillance at La Guardia Airport where I was looking for drugs in luggage, accompanied by a sniffer dog.

In those days I took up again with another of my police lovers, Bob Kelly, a homicide detective who had started a firm offering private investigation services and I began to work with him. He operated mainly out of the back of a van and for $400 a day he completed reports and carried out surveillance, recorded videos and took photos mostly for fraud cases for medical insurance but also for infidelities that were useful in divorce cases. That van was also our love nest.

Abandoned

At that time, Geraldine, Frank Smith's wife, was very ill. He had given me a gold ring once, saying that we would get married, but when we met one Wednesday, as we did on so many others, in the room that the police kept in the Marriot Hotel next to La Guardia Airport where we had met regularly for the last fifteen years, he was brutally cold.

'She died. Geraldine died. Don't even think about it. We're not getting married.'

I would only see him once more, in a car in the car park of the same hotel.

'I hate freeways, the cold and snow and so I'm going to retire and go to Florida to play golf for the rest of my life,' he announced.

'What about me? What about us?' I asked, crying at his unexpected decision and the fact that I would be a lot lonelier without him.

His reply is etched on my memory.

'It's not on the cards for us.'

And so he left me after a fifteen-year relationship without so much as a kiss, an embrace, or even a caress. I cried all night. I never saw him again. He is a bastard, but I miss him. He hurt me. And I hate him and love him at the same time. I feel stupid and deceived.

Good Memories

My heart was broken, although I also had my best memories of work during this period, a job I found by myself through an ad in the *New York Times.* It had nothing to do with surveillance or spying on anyone; instead I was looking after young girls with problems. It was a job in the Eufrasian Diagnostic Center, a place run by Catholic nuns in which, after embellishing my résumé, I was employed as a manager and I had to talk to and help teenagers who had been victims of rape or other attacks and were confronting addiction or depression and had left home or tried to commit suicide. It was not only a well-paid job, but I was proud of the respect that was shown to me by the twelve employees who reported to me. I could help and look after these girls in a way that I couldn't with my own daughter.

I was happy there until one day a nun who

ran the centre told me I had to leave. Taken aback, I asked why and she said that she couldn't give me a reason. I have always thought that someone who wanted me to lose that job had spoken to the nuns, perhaps telling them who I was and about my turbulent past, or the fact that I had never been to college. I was distraught and the only consolation I had was a new job in another field that I also liked, looking after animals. So I worked for the American Society for the Prevention of Cruelty to Animals, the ASPCA, for a while.

Other People Like Me

One day in 1987 Mark brought a book home for me, *On the Run,* written by Philip Agee. I didn't just read it, I devoured it. Something inside me was changing as I discovered in its pages that there were other people like me, people who had also done work for the CIA that weighed heavily on their conscience and hung over their lives. I looked for Agee and I knew that the United States had revoked his passport years ago. Although he lived in exile, he kept going and was trying to launch an association for people 'retired' from the Agency. Dave Mac-Michael, who headed up this group in the United States, sent me a ticket to Washington where, on 28 December 1987, I took part in a press conference to introduce the group which included people like the man who collaborated in the overthrow of the president of Guatemala and a retired agent who was sent to Cuba to poison milk, an act of terrorism that affected many children and grandparents on the island and made us cry when we heard his story.

It was liberating for us to be able to speak in public about what we had always had to keep secret and, for the press, it was an astonishing revelation. But it was also therapeutic to be able to expose the dissatisfaction with jobs and missions that caused moral conflicts within us and that weren't valued by the agencies and that they ignored us or treated us as if we were an embarrassment. I'm not the only one who didn't even receive a pension although I firmly believe that I deserved it. Luckily, I found a very united family of retired spies, a network where we could protect and help each other. MacMichael, for example, gave me $5,000 when Monica had a medical problem which could have cost her life and no hospital would take her because I didn't have insurance.

Setting Off for Hollywood

That press conference had a huge impact on us and one of the first to respond was Hollywood. They wanted to know what the government was up to and they didn't want a fictional film script but one that told the real story of the people who had lived through it body and soul. Oliver Stone asked to talk to us and paid for a trip to California plus $5,000 per person. So we ended up in an enormous mansion in the hills of Los Angeles where one of the first people I crossed paths with was the actress Daryl Hannah, who I didn't know or recognize at that time but then found out that she was going out with John John Kennedy, JFK's son, who would die tragically in 1999 in a plane crush. I have never been impressed by film stars but I had a very open conversation with her. When I confessed that I didn't know what to say, she encouraged me to speak simply and frankly about what had happened. I then went into the room and heard the other former agents telling their stories. When it was my turn, I said:

'I knew Castro. I'm a failed assassin.'

Some already knew my story because they had read a series of articles that were published in 1975 and applauded my account. The person I was most involved with and who I kept contact with was Oliver Stone himself who said he was interested in filming my story and even gave me $10,000 to send me to Germany to research my past and rediscover the first seven years of my life, although my naïve spirit and complete ignorance of how to manage business would betray me again.

In Germany I met a woman, Anna Meizner, who was working for a magazine. She was also interested in recounting my adventures and misadventures and asked me to sign a document which she said assured me was necessary to enable her to investigate my past. In good faith, I signed the document. Although Meizner did actually publish the article, it turned out that the document I had signed meant she could tell my life story. Without realising it, I had violated the agreement I had with Stone, who was furious, but he also put me onto his lawyer. In the end, he had to pay her $25,000 to cancel the contract. Although Oliver and I were still friends, it left a bitter taste in our relationship and the idea of making a film together evaporated. He still has material that I gave him, such as the photograph of Andrés that I found hidden in my mother's trunks when she died.

I tried to get more material by travelling to Cuba in 1988 but I couldn't get to see Fidel or recover any documents so I just spent ten days on holiday. I stayed in a small hotel, not at the Habana Libre, although I went there to eat. I met an attractive pilot, an Arab, who I went out with to party, and walked with him along the promenade. For the first time, I was just another tourist.

In Hollywood I met a couple of wonderful women who became great friends. One was Sarah, a multimillionaire, heir to a well-known company. The other was Laura, also a fabulous woman. They had met in rehab and I think they were in a relationship. In 1990, they were going to a large environmental conference in Nicaragua and I don't know why they had to cancel the trip but they asked me to go in their place. They had paid for everything for two people so I called Monica, who was then living in California, and invited her to come with me.

A Finger on the Trigger

I stayed in Miami with a good friend and activist, Linda, to get the plane tickets and vouchers for the hotel. She knew my story with Walters and when we went to a children's hospital in the city we saw his statue there. That greedy bastard, the man who had robbed my daughter and me of Marcos's money, had financed the construction of a block which had been named in his honour. Linda suggested that we tie a rope round the statue and pull it down with a car but I had a better idea. I always carried my gun with me. We went to the offices of Walters, Moore and Costanzo, his law firm, and I went up to his office. I walked in, closed the door and pointed the gun at him, demanding that he give me the money that he owed us. They only thing he took out of the safe was a copy of our trust fund agreement. When I told him I wanted to kill him, blow his brains out, his face went red. I think he wet himself. Perhaps he thought I was mad and would do it and I probably should have done it, but I preferred to leave him physically frightened.

'I'll be back,' I told him. 'You'll have to live your life looking over your shoulder each and every day of your life.'

Sometimes I feel I would have liked to have pulled the trigger that day but I didn't do it. The only consolation I have is that he had his own problems. His daughter was murdered and although he had contacts in the higher echelons of power and was even sent to the Vatican by President Jimmy Carter at the end of the 1970s, he had to tender his resignation when his law firm was investigated for fraud and the misappropriation of funds.

Traces of Andrés

When we arrived in Nicaragua, Monica and I took advantage of our stay to visit the Karl Marx Hospital in Managua, which was full of Germans. Talking with doctors and nurses, we found out that doctors from Cuba sometimes went there to look after children. We started asking if anyone knew a Cuban doctor called Andrés and they told us about an attractive young man who came from the island from time to time and helped mostly with child amputees. His name was Andrés Vásquez. I am convinced it was my son.

On that trip I also met Isabel Letelier, the widow of Orlando Letelier, the Chilean Ambassador to the United States, who was opposed to Augusto Pinochet's dictatorship and died in a car bomb in 1975 which was carried out by five members of the Cuban in Exile group, including the Novo brothers. Monica, who was a bodybuilder in those days and a finalist in the Miss Fitness USA competition and posed for *Playboy,* went to the gym with Christian, one of Isabel's four sons. She introduced me to Isabel and we became good friends. After the trip, Isabel introduced Monica to another of her sons, Francisco, and before long they were married, although the marriage didn't last long, and in 1991 Monica gave me my first grandchild, Matías, and I moved to California for a couple of months to help her.

When I returned home I rented an apartment in Queens opposite the one that Mark had rented and a little while later Monica and my grandson came to live with me. In those days I was working again on a new memoir that this time would be published. Thunder's Mouth Press, an icon of the counter-culture, the *underground* movement and progressivism, paid me $40,000 and had put me in touch with Ted Schwartzman, the writer appointed to help me. More than just a few memories would come out of that collaboration. One day I sent Monica to the editorial offices to deliver some photos that were to be used in the book. That was when she met Neil Ortenberg, the stepson of the fashion designer Liz Claiborne, who was running the publishing company. Shortly afterwards they were married.

More Rats in My Life

The book put me back in the news and a television company in Miami began to organise a meeting between Frank Sturgis and me on camera which was meant to be the staging of a peace agreement between the two of us, a truce. The Cubans in Miami threatened to release thousands of rats into the city if I went. They adored Frank and hated me, supposedly because of the failed attempt to kill Fidel with the pills, as it led to Sturgis's arrest in New York as a result of my testimony in Congress. If they hate me for anything, however, it's because I know too much about them and their dirty work. I know about so many things they were responsible for and so many of the crimes for which they were never convicted. George Bush, for example, released Luis Posada Carriles, who was responsible for the assassination of Letelier.

The meeting never took place. In December 1993, Sturgis died a couple of weeks after his sixty-ninth birthday. His lawyer confirmed that he had been a victim of cancer but I have always heard rumours of other stories and doubts about what really happened.

Defrauded

After squandering all the money from the book, I moved to Baltimore where Valerie now lived. She had opened a centre for the treatment of compulsive gamblers and she was investing in property. A famous director was interested in making a film about my life, and he had given me $25,000, which I put down on a house Valerie knew of in the area. It was a brownstone at 666 Washington Boulevard, in a part of town that at that time, the beginning of the 1990s, was a dangerous neighbourhood but today has become a very nice area. I put all my money into renovating the house and Mark, who had lost his job and had to give up his studies at university, came with me. He and I worked on that house nonstop for nine months, rebuilding everything. Suddenly, the former owner appeared, saying that he had an unpaid tax bill of $5,000 on the property. We didn't have any money so I asked Neil Ortenberg, who had come to see us with Monica, and although at first he said he wouldn't loan me the money he then changed his mind. Before I could do anything else, I was told that I had lost the house because I hadn't paid the debt. Mark and I, who had invested all my money and time there, had nothing left and we had to rent somewhere nearby. My son decided to go back to New York in 1995 and, as I had no means of keeping the rental property, I had to move in with my sister and start working with her in the treatment centre where I was in charge of patient admissions and I had to make sure all the beds were made and that the patients were given their medication.

One day while I was at work I had a fall. When I went to see the doctor at the Johns Hopkins Hospital, he took an X-ray and did a CAT scan which not only diagnosed a hip fracture but also degenerative arthritis. I signed up for Social Security and had three operations but something went wrong. It was practically impossible for me to walk because of a limp and going up three floors to my room was unthinkable. Mark hired a van and came to pick me up, collecting all my belongings and taking me to the apartment he had in Queens.

Then and to this day, Beegie was and has been my greatest support and after the hip replacement operation he began to take charge of everything and got me a special bed. Even so, I couldn't get hold of any money to pay the costs that were accumulating and I panicked when Social Security stopped covering me and I was left without any assistance for food. I was afflicted by severe physical pain and felt it was ridiculous and it went against my nature to be beholden to someone else or be held so low. I wanted to die and felt completely finished and at that point in my life, at nearly seventy years old I saw myself as so wounded that I would never be able to get up.

When I contacted the administration department at Social Security to find out why they had stopped covering me, they were surprised and said that someone had claimed $26,000 in my name. But the real surprise to me was that I had survived all that time without any means and I was on the point of being evicted. When I explained that I couldn't have collected that money because I was practically bedridden, and also that I wasn't in Baltimore but in New York, they sent someone to investigate who verified that I wasn't lying and that I couldn't even get to the door to answer it. It was obvious that I had been a victim of fraud and the inspector explained to me that it wasn't even recorded that I was living in the city because someone else was still collecting the money in Baltimore on my behalf. The authorities told me that they could press charges for fraud, but in the end, I never did get the money back.

Recompense

At that time, with eviction knocking on my door again, Mark, who was terrified and unable to help me, wrote a desperate letter to a senator for New York, Al D'Amato, who contacted a synagogue in our district. I wasn't a Jew but they made me feel part of the community because I had spent time in a concentration camp. One day, a rabbi appeared at the door. He hugged me and, overcome with emotion, cried on meeting a survivor. He not only gave me $6,000 and food, as well as paying the following year's rent on the apartment, but he made psychological care available to me. No one had ever treated me with such kindness and compassion.

At that time, Wilfried Huismann appeared in my life. He was a German reporter who called from Bremen and showed some interest in meeting me to make a documentary and write a book. Willy had heard rumours that I had died and when he visited me for the first time in autumn 1998 he found me only half alive, bedridden and unable to have the surgery I needed on my hip. We became friends immediately and he left me $10,000 for the operation. In those days, I had also received news from the Department of Justice of the United States in which they confirmed that I would receive compensation as a survivor of Bergen-Belsen. I had never imagined that I would be paid for being a prisoner but I received almost $80,000, $10,000 for every month in that terrible camp. The lawyer kept a tidy sum but it left me $30,000, enough to start again. I could breathe once more.

Back to Cuba, the Sea and Life

When Willy made his second journey from Germany, I had already had the surgery, thanks to his help, and I was in rehabilitation, so as soon as I could walk again he booked a trip. In March 2000, we flew to Cancún in Mexico and from there he, his team, my son Mark and I boarded the *Valtur Prima* and set sail for Havana. It was more than just a journalistic or documentary maker's project: for me it represented a return to ships and the sea. It signified a return to life.

On 5 March, we disembarked at the passenger terminal in Havana. I was back in Cuba, delighted but also weighed down with memories and emotions and I couldn't do much else other than look around and cry. I was still recovering from surgery but I could walk without a frame or a stick and I walked along the promenade, bought images of Che on a silver medallion and went back to the Habana Libre with Willy. We travelled to places like Isla Juventud (previously called Isla de Los Pinos or Los Pinos Island) where the Los Pinos prison had been situated.

We stayed at a small hotel in Havana and we were counting on permission from the regime to film but the request to interview Fidel was refused without explanation and Willy began to show signs of anxiety and annoyance. I had tried to find my son, Andrés, who we knew had worked as a paediatrician in Nicaragua as Andrés Vásquez, but I had no success. We hit a brick wall again trying to interview Fabián Escalante, the head of Cuban security. It became clearer by the minute that the film, which was called *Dear Fidel,* would not include any footage of my reunion with Castro, a remote possibility in any case but one which was completely buried when he decided to play his trump card and we went to interview Díaz Yáñez. I objected to the meeting because I wanted to keep a ray of hope alive, as small as that might be, that Fidel would meet me or come and see me and I knew that it would end everything if we went to see Yáñez, a man who had had his trust, an assistant who had even accompanied him to his meeting with Nixon but who had fallen from grace in 1960 and spent fifteen years in prison. It was only when we were on our way back to the port to return to Mexico that I accepted that we would go to see him.

Yáñez lived in an old and very dilapidated building that had undoubtedly been elegant in its day but which, like everything in Cuba today, is shabby and in need of a lick of paint. I was extremely happy to see him again and we hugged each other and cried. We shared memories and emotions but I didn't have much time and I had to leave.

Fidel, a Tremendous Son of a Bitch

When we returned to the ship, everyone was very upset and disappointed and I suggested to Willy that I write a letter to Fidel in which, for the first time in my life, I would dare to speak my mind, reminding him that I could have killed him twice and that I hadn't, while he, on the contrary, had not even deigned to help me to make a good film about what had happened. I didn't expect a response and, of course, I didn't get one but *Dear Fidel* was shown in cinemas and the book was in shops, libraries and kiosks, although Castro did everything possible to prevent the film being seen in some places, such as Mexico, where Willy says there was pressure not to show it.

What hurts me most is that filming that documentary was perhaps what cost Yáñez Pelletier his life. He was perfectly all right when we saw him in March 2000 but he died on 18 September that year. Even today, Willy thinks he was assassinated for seeing us and, although I will admit I'm not sure, I suspect that something like that is possible. For Fidel, you are either with him or against him. Steadfast. That's how he thinks, believing he's a king or a god, moved by jealousy, driven by fury if he thinks he has been betrayed. Even in old age, he can be a tremendous son of a bitch.

EPILOGUE:
I SHOULD BE HAPPY

Since that last trip to Cuba my life has just been about surviving. There have certainly been brilliant times, such as the trip to Germany in 2000 for the film premiere, but I came back and burned through the money I earned from that project all too quickly. I failed to buy a house in Brooklyn again and I had to live with Monica and her third husband in California for a couple of years. When I returned in 2004, I settled in College Point in Queens and had to have a hip operation. Thanks to Willy, I managed to get some money when he put me in touch with a Canadian producer who was interested in acquiring rights to make a film, but that was ten years ago and the project never happened. The only testimony to my life that exists on the big screen, apart from *Dear Fidel,* is *My Little Assassin,* a terrible film that was made for television in 1999, in which I am played by Gabrielle Anwar and

Joe Mantegna is Fidel.

Since 2007 I have lived in Queens in a cold ground-floor apartment which I rent from Marie, a Venezuelan woman who lives in the house with her dogs and dozens of cats. My days are restricted to taking my tablets, watching television — I like the history channels — and talking on the phone to my brother JoJo or to Valerie. Mark moved out a while ago but he is the person who continues to look after me. He takes me to the doctor and brings me my medicines or food. In 2014 Monica, Mark and I were invited by a Mr Ingo Mersemann to come to his Institute for Espionage, located in Oberhausen, Germany, to attend the opening of an exhibit about Love and Espionage that featured me and Monica and our relationship as mother and daughter. We had a wonderful visit where we took part in an onstage question and answer session with a room filled with reporters and other admirers, as well as a book signing afterwards where we all got to meet so many wonderful people. Monica now lives happily in beautiful Costa Rica, she has become an entrepreneur and an advocate for children's rights.

I am excited about a project for a musical based on Willy's book which is being produced in Amsterdam and my son was trying to find me a house in Germany to get me out of here. Anyway, Marie has said that I have to leave the apartment. I just want to leave this ice box; I just want somewhere to live.

It's true that I have had money in my life and that I have squandered it or managed it badly but I also think that I deserved a pension for all the jobs I did for the United States government, and I'm not just referring to the attempt to kill Fidel but to many other missions. I have helped bring criminals to justice, I have helped to bring babies into the world, I have saved lives and I have kept my mouth shut when it was necessary. All of this is part of being loyal to a country. The dereliction of duty made me even angrier when I know that half the guys who were selling drugs in Miami are getting $3,500 a month. It's not fair but I know that what has happened to me, this neglect, is part of a revenge pact. If you decide to take a step back from or even deviate slightly from their regulations, they take everything from you.

All I have now are what they call 'food stamps' that help me to buy food, Medicare and Medicaid which are the health care services for the old and the poor and $700 a month that I get from Social Security, of which $500 goes on rent. It's not fair and it's not enough.

I have no real friends or acquaintances that I can turn to. Many of those who could have helped me, mostly my lovers and acquaintances from the Mafia, are either dying or are no longer here. However, although I would never ask them for money, they would have offered it to me but I am, in any case, too proud to ask. I would prefer to starve to death.

I can't go back to family either. I have Mark, 'Beegie', I guess, but apart from him I don't feel I have any family. I don't say that as a reproach because I'm not very good at staying in touch. I have been a wanderer all my life and have lived without a permanent address for a long time. Nor do I say it with any angst. I don't miss it because I don't think I know what family is and what I don't know I can't miss. What is clear is that we never get together, we don't do things that families traditionally do such as getting together for Thanksgiving. We all go our own way.

Kiki succumbed to cancer, too young, in 1992. I love my brother JoJo, a sweet man who has never thrown anything back in my face and says quite sweetly that I am what I am. He and his wife send me presents at Christmas and sometimes shoes and coats as well. My wardrobe is full of new clothes that I don't wear because I have nowhere to go. Valerie has also become more of a presence in my life as well but when someone has deceived you there will always be something nagging somewhere in your mind that reminds you that you can't trust them.

I don't think love is on the cards for me either. I always liked to surround myself with good-looking men and I loved all my lovers but all I have now are memories. With Fidel, I lived a passion you can only have when you are nineteen years old, like an animal in heat. I was a young girl and I fell in love with him, his grandeur and his charisma. I was crazy about his eyes, his caresses . . . But I was like a David to his Goliath. He was so intense and charismatic that I was frightened of him, intimidated. He made you feel as if he was somewhere up here while you were down there in a place where it was impossible to truly know who he was. When I look at him now on the television, he's old and he looks sad. I would think that if he saw me now he would say the same about me.

I knew Marcos a little better and I loved him, too. I loved Eddie, but in a different way. Louis was basically a good man and, for a time, a great father to Mark. Perhaps the one who hurts most when I look back is Frank Smith, which was more of a physical dependence. The shock I felt when he left me and went to Florida comes back every time I think about him. I never did any harm to any of them intentionally but I accept that they disappeared from my life and faded away because of my errors. The only thing I can say is that I was stupid and haughty then, a rebel. I sleep with my dog now.

I look back and I can see clearly that sex was one of my weapons. A lot of people wanted to use me for their own purposes and sometimes I let them do it but I could also use it to make them sweat for it. I have had to be self-reliant. When I started working for Fiorini, I knew I was working in a man's world. In those days, there weren't any other female operatives. Sometimes they contracted a woman to complete a specific mission, to be a secretary, steal some information or spy on someone. None of them became friends. Then, when I started to get involved in the world of the Mafia, I couldn't talk to female friends in that circle about my work. I had to limit myself to conversations about men, clothes . . .

Perhaps because of that I miss Sturgis. I knew him for far too long. I always remember Lennie Small, the brute in *Of Mice and Men* by John Steinbeck. That's what he was like to me: a brute force, a man who wasn't educated or very intelligent or a bright star politically. He was a soldier obsessed with 'reds', communists, who played on almost all sides and risked my life. He was an assassin, dangerous but also predictable — at least he was to me. I knew him well and understood him. Today there are no more wars to fight. I am old and he isn't here any more. However, everything carries on as usual: interventions in foreign countries, shadowy operations, deceit and lying to the country . . . In fact, it is worse now and the United States is going backwards.

Writing this book has made me go back and think about it all, about everything that happened, everything I did and lived through. I know that many of the bad things that happened to me I did to myself. I'm very proud to have survived. I enjoyed some of the things that happened and I can look back and laugh. Sometimes I get depressed thinking about how unhappy I am and I feel old and alone. But when I am trapped by those thoughts I think to myself that I should go and do something productive, perhaps plant and care for a garden again. I am alive, weighed down by sorrow, but alive. I should be happy.

ABOUT THE AUTHOR

Marita Lorenz was born in Germany in 1939 and as a child, was interred in the Bergen-Belsen concentration camp. In the years that followed, she often sailed with her father (who was a ship captain) and, in 1959, she met Fidel Castro, with whom she fell in love. Later, the CIA would recruit and send her to assassinate Castro — an act she was unable to commit. She lives in Brooklyn, New York.

The employees of Thorndike Press hope you have enjoyed this Large Print book. All our Thorndike, Wheeler, and Kennebec Large Print titles are designed for easy reading, and all our books are made to last. Other Thorndike Press Large Print books are available at your library, through selected bookstores, or directly from us.

For information about titles, please call:
  (800) 223-1244

or visit our website at:
  gale.com/thorndike

To share your comments, please write:
  Publisher
  Thorndike Press
  10 Water St., Suite 310
  Waterville, ME 04901